LOST WORLDS AND MYSTERIOUS CIVILIZATIONS

El Dorado

LOST WORLDS AND
MYSTERIOUS CIVILIZATIONS

LOST WORLDS AND MYSTERIOUS CIVILIZATIONS

El Dorado

Dennis Abrams

CHELSEA HOUSE
An Infobase Learning Company

El Dorado
Copyright ©2012 by Infobase Learning

Chelsea House
An imprint of Infobase Learning
132 West 31st Street
New York NY 10001

Library of Congress Cataloging-in-Publication Data
Abrams, Dennis, 1960–
 El Dorado / by Dennis Abrams.
   p. cm. — (Lost worlds and mysterious civilizations)
 Includes bibliographical references and index.
 ISBN 978-1-60413-975-4 (hardcover)
 1. El Dorado—Juvenile literature. 2. America—Discovery and exploration—Juvenile literature.
 I. Title.
 E123.A24 2011
 979.4'41—dc22
                    2011011648

Chelsea House books are available at special discounts when purchased in bulk quantities for businesses, associations, institutions, or sales promotions. Please call our Special Sales Department in New York at (212) 967-8800 or (800) 322-8755.

You can find Chelsea House on the World Wide Web at http://www.infobaselearning.com

Text design by Erika K. Arroyo
Cover design by Alicia Post
Composition by EJB Publishing Services
Cover printed by Yurchak Printing, Landisville, Pa.
Book printed and bound by Yurchak Printing, Landisville, Pa.
Date printed: January 2012
Printed in the United States of America

10 9 8 7 6 5 4 3 2 1

This book is printed on acid-free paper.

All links and Web addresses were checked and verified to be correct at the time of publication. Because of the dynamic nature of the Web, some addresses and links may have changed since publication and may no longer be valid.

Contents

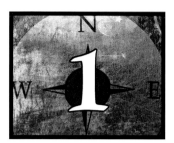

Gold Fever

Gold. The word alone is enough to get hearts racing. From South America in the 1500s, to the California gold rush of the late 1840s, up to the Great Mongolian Gold Rush of the last decade, whenever word has spread that there was gold to be found, men anxious to make their fortune were sure to follow.

But why gold? It is, after all, a metal just like any other. But somehow, gold is different. Its beauty, its satisfying weight and heft, its purity, its malleability, and its scarcity have all combined to give it a value far greater than its intrinsic worth. And that value has been recognized since the earliest days of man, as Jennifer Westwood wrote in *The Atlas of Mysterious Places*, quoted by Norma Gaffron in her book *El Dorado, Land of Gold*.

> *The powerful mystique of gold originally had much to do with its colour. The Egyptians linked [gold] to the sun and to the life-essence . . . In West Africa, [in ancient times] . . . a pinch of gold dust tucked into a man's loincloth was his passport through the spirit world.*

There is more to gold than just its color, mystique, and magic. For thousands of years, throughout the Western world, gold has equaled money. It has been made into coins and bars, it has been used as the basis of a nation's wealth, and a nation's currency is based on the amount of gold it holds in its treasuries. Whoever has gold, whatever nation controls the world's supply, is a nation that is both wealthy and powerful.

Placing such a value on gold is, however, a purely arbitrary decision; other societies, as we will see, have decided that a different item, a seashell, for example, is what has value. Gold is valuable simply because we agree that it is.

Its scarcity certainly added to its value, as did the fact that it was easy to work with and could be divided up into smaller units without losing its value. So it became clear that it was an ideal metal to be made into coins of equal weight. It was as early as 700 B.C. that gold coins were first introduced in Asia Minor, in the kingdom of Lydia in what is known today as Turkey.

From that point on, the quest for gold began in earnest in both fact and legend. In Greek mythology, Hercules was sent for his eleventh labor to the Garden of the Hesperides (in what is today Morocco) to bring back golden apples. Phoenicians from the coastal regions of what is now Israel, Lebanon, and Syria traveled as far as Spain to mine gold and bring it back home to be used in trade and commerce. The Bible says that King Solomon himself sent his ships down the Red Sea to Tarshish and Ophir (thought to be in today's India) to trade for gold (as well as for ivory, apes, and peafowls).

As successive empires came and went, the Western world's amassed gold horde continued to grow. The Persians absorbed the gold from the Babylonians, Egyptians, and Assyrians. The Greeks, under Alexander the Great, conquered the Persians, and their gold. And finally, the greatest empire of them all, the Roman Empire, absorbed into its boundaries all that had come before it, including the people, all their lands, and, naturally, their gold.

It was an empire built around military power and economic power backed by gold. The early Roman stern morality and piety quickly developed into a lust for wealth and gold at all costs. As the Roman poet Sextus Propertius wrote, quoted by Robert Silverberg in his book *The Golden Dream: Seekers of El Dorado*, "Men now worship gold to the neglect of the gods. By gold good faith is banished and justice is sold."

By most reckonings, the high point of the Roman Empire was during the reign of Augustus Caesar. When he died, in A.D. 14, the Roman gold supply might have been as large as 500,000,000 ounces (14,174,760 kilograms). But there were signs of difficulties to come. Romans continued

When European countries began to colonize regions around the world, Spain set its sights on South America. There, Spanish conquistadors discovered civilizations filled with gold, and rumors of an even bigger city built of the precious metal created the legend of El Dorado. *Above*, pre-Hispanic gold relics from Peru.

to work the same mines in Spain as had the Phoenicians, mining them until there was virtually nothing left. And there still wasn't enough gold to maintain the empire.

But that treasury was soon emptied, as the gold moved eastward to purchase, among other things, Chinese silks. That in itself wouldn't have been a problem, but at the same time, barbarian invasions of its own empire cut Rome off from its sources of additional gold. The gold of the Romans, the basis of their power and wealth, soon either disappeared into private hands, was stolen by invading Goths and Vandals, or just simply disappeared.

By A.D. 800 , the total amount of recoverable gold throughout Europe, the basis of its currency, had plunged to less than one-tenth of what had been available during the time of Augustus Caesar. This lack of gold made trade nearly impossible, kept prices low, and was a factor that contributed to the period commonly known as the Dark Ages.

Gradually, though, Europe emerged from the Dark Ages. And, like a baby waking up from a long nap it began to slowly explore the world around it. Old mines that had long been unused were reopened, and new ones were discovered. Advances in ships and navigation made it possible for the kingdoms of Europe to refill their treasuries by sailing abroad.

It fell to the Portuguese to make the first major steps outside of Europe. Prince Henry the Navigator sent his ships farther and farther down the west coast of Africa, until in 1488 Bartolomeu Dias sailed around the Cape of Good Hope at Africa's southernmost point, proving that there was a sea route to India and its riches. Dias never made it to India, but in 1495, Vasco de Gama did, sailing around Africa to India. By doing so, he opened up a new world of trade and made, temporarily at least, Portugal the dominant world power.

But while Portugal was looking to the east, Spain was looking west in search of gold and riches. The story of El Dorado is largely a story of the Spanish and their search for gold—a story that begins with two familiar names, King Ferdinand and Queen Isabella, and their need for gold to rebuild their country.

THE SPANISH NEED GOLD

Since the eighth century, Spain had been controlled by the Moors, Muslims who had crossed over from North Africa. Gradually though, the Christians pushed back against the Moorish invasion, and under the joint rule of the married King Ferdinand of Aragon and Queen Isabella of Castile (who governed two distinct kingdoms within the geographic territory of Spain), Granada, the last territory within Spain under Moorish control, fell on January 2, 1492.

But nearly 800 years of war between Moors and Christians had left the country desperately poor and isolated from the rest of the world. Spain's dry climate made agriculture difficult, and its mountainous terrain made trade and commerce even more so. Spain needed gold to rebuild, and Queen Isabella in particular needed money both to maintain her power and sweep Spain clean of all Muslim and non-Christian influences, using the power of the Spanish Inquisition to enforce her policies and expelling all Jews from the country.

It should come as no surprise, then, that when an Italian sailor from Genoa named Christoforo Colombo (known to history as Christopher Columbus) arrived at the court of Queen Isabella with promises of wealth to be found, he ultimately found a receptive audience. To sail around Africa going east to get to the riches of India, China, and Japan was a long and dangerous journey. Columbus assured Isabella that by sailing west, across the Ocean Sea (today known as the Atlantic) he'd find a direct route

The ancient civilizations in South America, such as the Inca in Peru, were advanced in science, mathematics, and agriculture. They were also skilled in metalworking and used gold to make items for religious rituals. Above, a ceremonial gold mask from Peru.

to the wealth of Asia. And along the way, he promised her, he'd find lands that he could claim in her name and large numbers of "heathens" he could convert to Christianity.

There was no way she could say no. Of course, Columbus was wrong. There was no direct route to Asia. Instead, there were two unknown continents, North and South America, directly in his path. Even so, the riches that he found were enough to start a frenzied exploration of the New World. Explorer after explorer decided to take a chance and leave the life they had always known to sail across the Atlantic in search of fame, fortune, and gold.

It was, in fact, the age of the quest; the search for treasures beyond imagination; the search for mythical kingdoms that may or may not have ever existed. Men went out in search of Prester John, the legendary Christian king whose realm was first thought to be in India, then in central Asia, and then in Ethiopia before the realization finally set in that it was all just a myth. Men went in search of the mythical lost island of Atlantis. They went searching for King Solomon's mines at Ophir. For the seven Cities of Cibola. For the Fountain of Youth. For the Holy Grail. For the land of the women warriors known as the Amazons.

But mostly they went out in search for treasure, for gold, specifically in the newly discovered worlds of South America. As their explorations continued, and as the Spanish conquistadors discovered and conquered the lands of the Aztecs and the Incas, finding wealth and riches beyond their imaginations, stories began to surface of even richer lands to be found, of gold beyond belief. Stories were heard of the land of the Golden Man, a land always to be found just over the next mountain range, past the next river, a land that came to be known as El Dorado.

As Robert Silverberg summed it up in his book *The Golden Dream: Seekers of El Dorado,*

> *The quest for El Dorado was an enterprise of fantasy that obsessed the adventurers of Europe for more than a century. Tales of a golden kingdom and a golden king, somewhere in the unexplored wilderness of South America, spurred men on to notable achievements of endurance, chivalry, and—too often—crime. Nothing halted the pursuers of the golden dream, neither snow-capped mountains nor blazing plains, neither the thin air of lofty plateaus nor the green intricacy of*

steaming tropical jungles. They marched on, killing and plundering, suffering incredible torments, often traveling—as one chronicler put it—con el alma en los dientres, with their souls between their teeth.

What were the stories that drove these explorers to such heroic feats and such desperate crimes? What did the explorers find on their quest? Were the stories of El Dorado true? Was it myth? Legend? Reality? A combination of all three? The true story of the search for El Dorado is in many ways even more interesting than the legend that surrounds it, and it begins on October 12, 1492. That was the date Christopher Columbus landed in the Bahamas and decided that he had found the outlying island of the Indies and that the fabulous wealth of Asia, and the golden kingdoms of his dreams, were within his reach.

The Search Begins

When Christopher Columbus sailed from Palos de Frontera, Spain, on August 3, 1492, he left with the firm conviction that by sailing west he would come to the Orient. He even carried with him on his voyage a copy of a letter from Paolo Toscanelli, a noted Italian mathematician and astronomer, telling the king of Portugal that a ship sailing westward from Europe would reach the lands of the Great Khan, seen in the west as the ruler of China and its surrounding lands.

And, he had undoubtedly read Marco Polo's book describing his trip to China and his description of it, cited by John Hemming, as "a country richer than any other yet discovered . . . It possesses gold and silver and precious stones and all kinds of spices in large quantities—things which do not reach our countries at present." Polo went on to describe the city of Quinsay (Hangchow), the home of ten bridges built entirely of marble, the province of Cathay (around today's Beijing), the home of the Great Khan, and the island of Cipangu (Japan), a land unknown to the West "very rich in gold, pearls and precious stones, with temples and palaces covered in gold."

As important as spices and silver and precious stones were, as important as finding new lands was, as important as working to convert the heathens he knew he'd find to Christianity, gold was at the heart of his search. Quoted by Gaffron, Columbus wrote:

> *Gold is the most exquisite of all things . . . Whoever possesses gold can acquire all that he desires in this world. Truly, for gold he can gain entrance for his soul into paradise.*

One can only imagine his feelings when he landed in the Bahamas on October 12, 1492, and was greeted by a gathering of naked people. Columbus was not one to be daunted by what he saw before him, however. He wrote in his journal the next day, quoted by Gaffron:

> *At daybreak great multitudes of men came to the shore, all young and of fine shapes, and very handsome . . . [They came to the ships in small canoes] loaded with balls of cotton, parrots, javelins, and other things too numerous to mention. These they exchanged for whatever we chose to give them. I was very attentive to them [and] strove to learn if they had any gold. Seeing some of them with little bits of metal hanging at their noses, I gathered from them by signs that by going southward or steering round the island in that direction, there would be a king who possessed great cups of gold. I tried to get them to go there but found they were unacquainted with the route.*

Christopher Columbus was the first but not the last Spanish explorer to be convinced that the gold he was looking for was to be found by traveling just a little bit farther.

CIPANGU?

He quickly set sail, going out in search for the island the Indians had pointed him to; one the Indians called "Colba," one that he was certain was Cipangu, what today we call Japan. He was wrong. One week later, Columbus made landfall at Colba, which turned out to be the island of Cuba. There, he was told that it took ten days to sail to the mainland, where he was determined, as quoted by Hemming, to go "to the city of Quinsay, to present the letters from Your Highnesses to the Great Khan . . . "

Columbus continued to travel throughout the Caribbean (pioneering, as author Robert Silverberg suggested, the Caribbean cruise), searching everywhere for news of the Great Khan. He stopped at island after island, planting crosses as he went and claiming the land, despite the fact that it was already inhabited, for Spain.

He landed on San Salvador. He landed on Hispaniola (the island now occupied by two countries, Haiti and the Dominican Republic). There, a messenger arrived with gifts from a nearby king. One of the gifts was a

When he arrived in the Bahamas, Columbus believed that he had reached Asia and referred to the local indigenous people as Indians. Columbus was eager to find a source of treasure and learned from these Indians that he must travel south for gold.

mask covered with hammered gold. The messenger assured Columbus that the king lived near where the gold could be found.

Columbus was unable to make his way there, but, with trading, he was certain that he had collected enough gold to convince Queen Isabella to finance another expedition to the New World. Leaving 39 of his men on the island to collect gold from the mines he was certain they were to find in his absence, he set sail for Spain on January 4, 1493.

Queen Isabella was indeed pleased with the news and claimed the Indies as possessions of the Castilian crown, adding that all expeditions and exploration of the New World could only be conducted under license (with the permission) of the crown of Castille. That same year, Pope Alexander VI confirmed Isabella's claim and then went one step further by simply dividing the world between Spain and Portugal by drawing a line from pole to pole, about a hundred miles (160 kilometers) west of the Azores. Everything that was east of that line was given to Portugal for its exclusive use; the land west of that line went to Spain.

Columbus made three additional voyages to the New World, never finding his promised route to the wealth of China, India, and Japan, and never finding the rich gold mines he was sure would be his. On his last trip to the Americas in 1502, still reluctant to admit that he had found not Asia but a new unknown continent, he met a fleet of 30 Spanish ships at Santo Domingo, Hispaniola, returning to Spain well aware that they were in a new land, loaded with West Indian gold—one ship contained a nugget of gold that is said to have weighed 30 pounds (14 kg)! The land that Columbus had "discovered" had within just ten years become an important source of gold for Spain, as expedition after expedition and explorer after explorer pressed farther and farther into Central and South America.

In 1501, Rodrigo de Bastidas, a Spanish merchant from Seville, and Juan de la Cosa, a former navigator with Columbus, had visited the northern coast of what is now South America, discovering and naming the harbor of Cartagena. There, they established relations with the natives and sent goodly amounts of golden objects back to Spain. Christoval Guerra and Pedro Niño explored the Venezuelan coast and went to Spain with gold and pearls, as well as the news that while gold was relatively scarce on South America's northern coast, it was more abundant farther to the west. King Ferdinand was so pleased with the news that in 1508, he authorized the first attempts at establishing permanent settlements on the mainland. The main task of the settlers, naturally, was to search for gold mines for Spain.

As John Hemming wrote in *The Search for El Dorado*, "The ultimate dream of every conquistador was to discover a gold or silver mine that would yield a steady flow of treasure." Obviously, there were other goals as well: a new life, a route to Asia and its spices, the desire to spread Christianity, the search for an El Dorado or paradise, but underlying it all was the search for gold and treasure, and nothing would be allowed to stop anyone in their search.

As the New England historian William H. Prescott wrote in his masterpiece *History of the Conquest of Peru*, quoted by Robert Silverberg:

> *Gold was the incentive and the recompense, and in the pursuit of it [the Spaniard's] inflexible nature rarely hesitated as to the means. His courage was sullied with cruelty, the cruelty that flowed equally— strange as it may seem—from his avarice and his religion ... The Castillian, too proud for hypocrisy, committed more cruelties in the*

THE ARREST AND TRIAL
OF CHRISTOPHER COLUMBUS

Although Christopher Columbus may have been one of the bravest explorers the world has ever known, his skills as a governor left much to be desired. Returning to Spain after his first voyage to the New World, Columbus was named governor and viceroy of the Indies. But by 1499, Columbus, in poor health and faced with accusations of governing in a tyrannical manner, sent two ships to Spain, asking the court to appoint a royal commissioner to help him govern.

Francisco de Bobadilla was sent by the court. But instead of offering assistance, he was given total control as governor. He arrived in Santo Domingo while Columbus was away and was immediately informed that the three Columbus brothers, Christopher, Bartolome, and Diego, were guilty of atrocities against their own men as well as the native population. When Columbus returned, he had manacles placed on his arms and chains on his feet and was thrown into prison until he could be returned to Spain. He was 53 years old.

On October 1, 1500, Columbus and his brothers were sent back home to Spain. Upon arriving in Cadiz, a heartbroken Columbus wrote to a friend at court:

It is now seventeen years since I came to serve these princes with the Enterprise of the Indies. They made me pass eight of them in discussion, and at the end rejected it as a thing of jest.

name of religion than were ever practiced by the pagan idolater or the fanatical Moslem.

The next century of exploration, one in which explorer after explorer traveled through Central and South America in search of gold and glory, would also be a century of suffering and death for the region's original inhabitants, as the conquistadors' quest for wealth, combined with their

Nevertheless I persisted therein ... Over there I have placed under their sovereignty more land than there is in Africa and Europe, and more than 1,700 islands ... In seven years I, by the divine will, made that conquest. At a time when I was entitled to expect rewards and retirement, I was incontinently arrested and sent home loaded with chains ... The accusation was brought out of malice on the basis of charges made by civilians who had revolted and wished to take possession on the land ... I beg your graces, with the zeal of faithful Christians in whom their Highnesses have confidence, to read all my papers, and to consider how I, who came from so far to serve these princes ... now at the end of my days have been despoiled of my honor and my property without cause, wherein is neither justice nor mercy.

During his trial, 23 witnesses testified that Christopher Columbus made regular use of torture while governing Hispaniola.

Columbus and his brothers remained in prison for six weeks before King Ferdinand ordered their release. Not long afterward, the king and queen brought Columbus and his brothers to the court in Granada. There, after hearing the brothers' pleas, their freedom and wealth was restored to them, and, after much negotiating, the royal couple agreed to fund Columbus's fourth and final voyage to the New World. His days of governorship, however, were over.

desire to spread the word of Christ, led to the annihilation of anyone who refused to surrender their gold to the Spanish, or their souls to the Christian god.

FINDING THE PACIFIC

In 1509, the Spanish explorer Vasco Núñez de Balboa, who had been living on the island of Hispaniola and going deeper and deeper in debt, stowed away on a ship heading for the South American coast. One year later, Balboa, along with soldiers he had recruited along the way, founded the first permanent Spanish settlement in the New World, located in what is today the country of Panama. He called it Santa Maria la Antigua del Darien.

The settlement didn't come without a price—the native inhabitants first had to be conquered and defeated. In the process of doing so, Balboa and his men took possession of, as quoted by Silverberg, "plates of gold, such as they hang on their breasts and other parts, and other things, all of them amounting to ten thousand pesos of fine gold." Ten thousand pesos worth, though, was apparently just the beginning.

When the gold was being weighed out, it is said that a young man who was there hit the scales with his fist and angrily told Balboa that "If this is what you prize so much that you are willing to leave your distant homes, and risk even life itself for it, I can tell you of a land where they eat and drink out of golden vessels, and gold is as cheap as iron is with you." Balboa had explored the Rio Atrato and surrounding rivers, determined to find the territory of a *cacique* (chieftain) named Dabeiba. He never made it to the land of Dabeiba, but what he learned gave him even greater impetus to explore farther, as he wrote in a letter to King Ferdinand II, quoted by Gaffron:

> *Many Indians who have seen it tell me that this cacique Dabeiba has certain baskets of gold, and that it requires the whole strength of a man to get these onto his shoulders. This cacique gets the gold from some distance away, in the mountains, and the manner by which he gets it is thus: two days' journey away, there is a beautiful land where the people are very Carib and bad. They eat as many humans as they can get ... They are the owners of these mines, which, according to the news I have heard, are the richest in the world ... There are two methods of collecting the gold, without any effort. One is to wait until the streams have risen in the ravines, and then, when the floods have passed and the river beds are dry again, the gold is exposed, having been washed out from the banks and carried from the mountains in very sizeable nuggets ... Another way of collecting gold is to await the time when the vegetation has dried in the mountains and then set it on fire. After the burning, they go and look in the heights and in the most likely places, and they collect it in great quantity and in*

fine nuggets. The Indians who collect this gold, bring it in grains, just as they find it, in order to have it melted, and they trade it with this cacique Dabeiba. In exchange he gives them boys and girls to eat, and women to serve them as wives, whom they do not eat. He also gives them peccaries [a variety of wild pig] of which there are many in this land, and much fish, cotton cloths, and salt, and also such objects of worked gold as they desire. These Indians trade only with the cacique Dabeiba, and nowhere else . . . This cacique Dabeiba has a great place for melting gold in his house, and he has a hundred men continuously working gold.

Were the stories that Balboa had heard true? Were they legend? Were the people telling him stories that they thought he wanted to hear? In some ways it really doesn't matter what was true because the stories were believed. The New World was obviously a land of dangers, but, to a man of

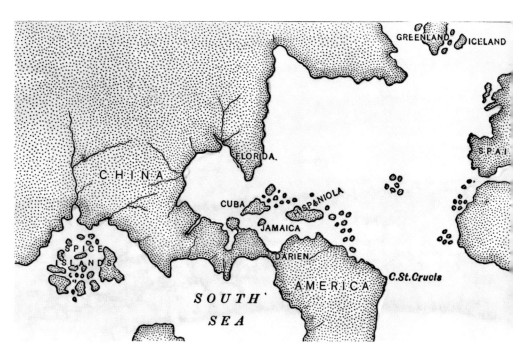

Before the New World was discovered, people believed that Asia was on the other side of the Atlantic Ocean. After Columbus and Balboa returned from their expeditions, Europeans amended their maps to reflect their new belief that China, and the rest of Asia, was attached to the Americas.

bravery and courage, there was clearly gold to be found in nearly unbeliev-able quantities.

They weren't yet stories of El Dorado—those were still to come. But stories of greater and greater amounts of gold to be had were already beginning to work their magic, drawing explorers farther and farther away from the coast, and deeper and deeper into the jungles.

Balboa sent word to King Ferdinand of what he had learned on his expedition. In a letter from January 1513, quoted by Silverberg, he told his king that he had found "great secrets of marvelous riches," speaking of "many rich mines . . . gold and wealth with which a great part of the world can be conquered. I have learned it in various ways, putting some to the torture, treating some with love and giving Spanish things to come." He asked Ferdinand for weapons, supplies, materials, and 1,000 men from the island of Hispaniola to assist him on his search for gold.

Like most who ask for assistance, he didn't get everything he wanted. But, with the support of 190 Spaniards and a group of local guides, he traveled by ship from Darien to the narrowest part of the Isthmus of Pan-ama, where just 60 miles (96 km) of land divided the Atlantic Ocean from the Pacific. From there, the overland trek began. Hostile tribes were dealt with, either by diplomacy or force, until, on September 25, 1513, Balboa, going alone, came to the top of the final hill and gazed down upon the Pacific Ocean, in a moment memorialized more than 300 years later by the British poet John Keats:

> He star'd at the Pacific—and all his men
> Look'd at each other with a wild surmise—
> Silent, upon a peak in Darien.

It was a historic moment. Vasco Núñez de Balboa was the first Euro-pean to see the Pacific Ocean from the New World. The geographic riddle of the Americas had been solved, and now the Spanish had the means to explore the western coast of South America as they had already begun to do in the east. And it was in the west, or so the Spanish were told, that gold beyond their reckoning could be found. The age of exploring, conquering, and plundering was about to begin in earnest.

The End of Two Empires

In 1518, Diego de Velasquez, who had been with Columbus on his voyages, was now the ruler of Cuba. It was Velasquez who selected Hernán Cortés to assemble and lead an expedition consisting of 11 ships, 500 men, 13 musketeers, 32 crossbowmen, 16 horses, and 7 toy-sized cannons. Their mission? To conquer Mexico for the Spanish crown.

Unfortunately for Velasquez, he had come to the conclusion too late that Cortés was too ambitious for himself and all together too untrustworthy to trust with command of the mission. Cortés and his men had left Cuba, landing on the Yucatan Peninsula in March of 1519, immediately claiming it for Spain. By July he had taken over Vera Cruz. There, emissaries from Montezuma, the ruler of the Aztec Indian Empire, led by Teuhtlilli, came to learn more about the strange white men who had arrived by sea. Some preliminary trading was done, and Teuhtlilli left with gifts for Montezuma, returning to Vera Cruz one week later, accompanied by 100 men and gifts that awed and amazed all who saw them.

Bernal Diaz del Castillo, who was with Cortés, described what he saw in his book *The Discovery and Conquest of Mexico*, as quoted by Norma Gaffron. Among the gifts received from Montezuma were:

> *... a wheel like a sun, as big as a cartwheel, with many sorts of pictures on it ... the whole of fine gold ... another wheel ... of greater size made of silver of great brilliancy in imitation of the moon with other figures shown on it ... and the chief brought back the helmet full of fine grains of gold.*

And there was more.

> *Next came twenty golden ducks, of fine workmanship, some orna-*
> *ments in the shape of their native dogs, many others in the shapes of*
> *tigers, lions, and monkeys, ten necklaces of very fine workmanship,*
> *some pendants. They brought crests of gold, plumes of rich, green*
> *feathers, silver crests . . . [and] models of deer in hollow gold.*

Nothing could have pleased Cortés more. An empire that could produce gifts of gold in such abundance must be very wealthy and have gold
mines of its own as the source of its wealth. The next year, with the assistance of indigenous peoples he had converted to his side, including the
woman known as La Malinche, who spoke Aztec and Mayan, as well as
Spanish, he and his men set out to make history.

When they arrived at the Aztec capital of Tenochtitlan on November
8, 1519, in what is today Mexico City, they found a city of great wealth,
a city of marvels, a city that seemed to be more mythical than real, as
described by eyewitness Bernal Diaz del Castillo.

> *When we saw so many cities and villages built in the water and other*
> *great towns on dry land, and that straight and level causeway going*
> *towards Mexico, we were amazed and said it was like the enchanted*
> *houses described in the legend of Amadis, on account of the great*
> *towers and buildings rising from the water, all built of masonry.*
> *Some of our soldiers even asked whether the things we saw were not*
> *a dream? It is not surprising that I describe it here in this way, since*
> *there is much to ponder and I do not know how to tell it; for we saw*
> *things never before heard of or seen or even dreamed!*

By August of 1521 the Aztec Empire was no more. Cortés and his small
army had defeated the once powerful Montezuma with a combination
of luck, advanced weapons, diplomacy, and diseases that quickly spread
from the Spanish to the Aztecs, who had no natural defenses against them.
Ships laden with gold and other treasures taken from the defeated Aztec
Empire soon arrived in Spain, along with inspiration for other would-be
explorers. Here, at last, was proof, as John Hemming put it, that beyond
the unpromising coasts of the New World lay the possibility of conquest of
kingdoms of unimagined wealth.

Spanish explorer Hernán Cortés left Europe with the intent of taking over Mexico for his country. As he began claiming Mexican lands for Spain, the Aztecs sent him gifts of gold and invited him to visit their capital city, Tenochtitlan. There, Cortés met the Aztec king Montezuma (*above*).

THE SEARCH CONTINUES

Earlier expeditions in search of golden kingdoms had ended up in disappointment, finding little more than islands whose naked inhabitants owned just a few trinkets of gold. Cortés, on the other hand, had stumbled onto the mother lode, and, with just a hundred men had conquered an empire and made his fortune. Were there other Mexicos, other Aztec Empires to be found in the unexplored territories of the Americas, just waiting for the brave and daring? To the Spanish, the New World of the Americas was a land of infinite possibilities where, because so much of it was still unknown, anything was still possible.

Spanish men, driven by ambition and greed, set sail for the New World by the hundreds. Using Darien as their starting point, expeditions moved upward into Central America and downward into South America. From the heart of Cortés's Mexico they spread through the country in search of gold and then began moving north, toward the American Southwest. Florida was "discovered" on April 2, 1513, by the Spanish conquistador Ponce de León who, legend has it, was searching for the "Fountain of Youth."

By 1525, so many Spaniards had left their home in search of gold that the Venetian ambassador to Spain, Andrea Navagiero, wrote of his shock at how sparse Spain's population had become. "Seville," he wrote, quoted by Silverberg, "was left almost to the women." The lure of gold, it seems, was strong enough to cause people to risk their lives on the hope of finding it.

And many of them did find it. Gold, for example, was found at the mouth of the Rio de Plata, located between modern-day Uruguay and Argentina. And it wasn't just Spaniards who were out looking for gold. Cortés's letters describing what he had found in Mexico had been published in Nuremberg, Germany, the home base for the Welser Company, whose very business was in overseas trade.

Traditionally, the company had dealt in spices such as ginger, pepper, nutmeg, and cinnamon from India and Ceylon, as well as fabrics from other locations. Its primary interest in the New World had been in the bark of the guaiacum tree, which grew in the West Indies and was used as a medicine. But with the news of Cortés's gold, whole new avenues of possibilities seemed to be opening up.

The Welser family was in an enviable position to take advantage of the wealth to be found in the New World. Powerful and rich on their own,

THE ARRIVAL OF MONTEZUMA

In his book, *The Discovery and Conquest of Mexico*, author and eye-witness Bernal Diaz del Castillo describes the magnificent arrival of the Aztec emperor, Montezuma.

The Great Montezuma got down from his litter, and those great Caciques supported him with their arms beneath a marvellously rich canopy of green coloured feathers with much gold and silver embroidery and with pearls and chalchihuites suspended from a sort of bordering, which was wonderful to look at. The Great Montezuma was richly attired according to his usage, and he was shod with sandals, the soles were of gold and the upper part adorned with precious stones. The four Chieftains who supported his arms were also richly clothed according to their usage, in garments which were apparently held ready on the road to enable them to accompany their prince, for they did not appear in such attire when they came to receive us. Besides these four chieftains, there were four other great Caciques who supported the canopy over their heads, and many other Lords who walked before the Great Montezuma, sweeping the ground where he would tread and spreading cloths on it, so that he should not tread on the earth. Not one of these Chieftains dared even to think of looking him in the face, but kept their eyes lowered with great reverence, except for those four relations, his nephews, who supported him with their arms.

they had recently made a loan of 141,000 gold ducats to Charles V, king of Spain and Holy Roman Emperor. As a way of saying "thanks," Charles gave the Welser family the governorship of the territory of Venezuela. This position entitled them to conquer the native inhabitants to be found there and take whatever treasures they found there for themselves, just turning over the normal one-fifth of all profits to the king. "It was," said author Victor von Hagen, quoted by Gaffron, "the beginning of another 'journey to the Golden Man.'"

The expedition was led by Ambrosius Ehinger, who, arriving in South America heard the first vague stories of a fabulous city of gold, a place where gold was so plentiful that the body of their chief was powdered with it. But, like most explorers of the time, he had little to no idea just how vast the South American continent was. And so, when he began his journey in 1529, he had little idea of the dangers facing him and his men.

Traveling through the land of the Jirajaras, the expedition was constantly harassed by warriors armed with six-foot-long (1.8 meters) poisoned arrows. Occasionally the fighting would stop long enough for some trading to take place. Ehinger's men offered the Jirajaras knives, scissors, and other German products in exchange for badly needed food. But the Jirajaras barely had enough food for themselves, and the men found themselves living on the hearts of chonta plants and on giant beetle grubs, supplemented whenever possible with crocodile and iguana tails, which, as the expedition's translator later wrote, "when skinned and prepared, were edible."

The expedition lasted eight months, and the explorers made it no farther than the site of the future city of Maracaibo, where Ehinger left behind a small garrison along with those too ill from fever to travel back to the coast. Returning to Coro, Ehinger began preparing for his next expedition, raising money by shipping off branded Venezuelan Indians to be sold as slaves in Santo Domingo. By 1531 Ehinger was ready to depart Coro once again, accompanied by several hundred Spaniards and a large number of Indian bearers, whose job was to carry the Spaniards' supplies.

The march, which made it as far inland as the Rio Cesar, faced native inhabitants not eager to have Spanish troops, already known for their cruelty, travel through their lands. Ehinger met their opposition with brute force and extraordinary cruelty, wiping out entire villages as a lesson to the rest not to resist his men. Bartolome de las Casas, as quoted by Silverberg wrote that Ehinger attacked the locals "without comparison a great deal more cruelly than any other tyrants of which we have spoken for," proving himself "more unnatural and fierce than raging tigers, or wolves, or ramping lions."

It seems based on all accounts that Ehinger's march through Venezuela in search of gold should best be remembered for its astonishing atrocities. Native inhabitants who came to meet the troops with gifts were attacked and cut to pieces. Chieftains were made into slaves to intimidate their tribes. Any captives that rebelled were burned alive in thatch huts.

But these tactics, brutal as they were, did achieve the desired results. By the end of the outward leg of the expedition, Ehinger had amassed 600 pounds of gold (60,000 *pesos de oro*), a large quantity of precious stones, and enough slaves to carry it all back to the coast. The slaves were in chains, each linked to the next by metal rings around their necks. The problem with that setup, though, was that in order to release one slave from the chains, all had to be released.

For the Spanish conquistadors this proved to be more trouble than it was worth. Ehinger gave instructions that if any slave tired, or was unable to go on, he was to be severed from the chain by the simple process of having his head cut off. And since the lives of their Indian slaves were cheap and the gold had to be carried, it seems that there was a literal trail of native inhabitants' heads lining their march.

Although many of the tribes were hostile, one, the Pacabueyes, proved to be the tribe of the conquistadors' dreams. They greeted the Spaniards peacefully, and better yet, they had gold, and lots of it. Within eight days of gift giving and trading, the Spaniards had amassed an additional 91 kilos (200 pounds) of gold.

The expedition moved on, encountering other tribes, killing as they went, and amassing even more gold. For the Spanish, it seemed that no amount of gold was ever enough. In fact, Ehinger decided that there was too much gold to leave the area immediately. He sent his lieutenant, Inigo de Vascuna, along with 24 other men, back to Coro with the expedition's gold along with orders to return with reinforcements to conquer and colonize the area. Ehinger and his remaining men returned to Pacabuey country and used it as a base to further explore the region.

What seemed a most successful expedition quickly turned into a disaster, due, in no small part, to Ehinger's unwillingness to attempt to make peace or even to communicate with any of the local tribes. If he had, he would have learned that within just a few days' march was the northern territory of the Muisca, the Chibcha people whose wealth, once it was discovered, would inspire part of the legend of El Dorado.

Instead, Spaniards began dropping like flies as disease took its toll. Ehinger himself, under attack in the village of Chinacota by the survivors of an earlier Spanish attack, was hit in the neck by a poison arrow. He

Stories of Cortés's conquests reached Spain and created a frenzy of greed. Men set sail for South America and began slashing their way across the continent in search of more gold and bigger treasure. *Above*, one of the few gold Inca statues that was not melted down by Spaniards.

survived for only four days before dying, as described in a letter quoted by Hemming, "delirious and raving from the poison in the deserted village of the tribe that killed him." The rest of Ehinger's men continued on their way, killing the local inhabitants as they went, burning their villages, and trying to find their way back to Coro, all the while wondering what happened to Inigo de Vascuna. Why hadn't he returned with supplies and reinforcements?

Along the way, they came across something they did not expect to see: a man with distinctly Spanish features, naked except for a feathered crown, carrying a bow and arrow. The man was Francisco Martin, and, as it turned out, he was the sole survivor of Vascuna's expedition, and he had an equally horrible tale to tell. His expedition had gotten lost. Disease and hunger had knocked the men off one by one, leaving only Martin, who, left behind when his feet were being eaten by worms, had been taken in and cared for by a local tribe, living, during his year with them, as an Indian.

In November 2, 1533, two years after they had left, the ragged survivors of the expedition arrived back in Coro, leaving little but death and destruction in their path. But what happened to the gold that Ehlinger had sent back to Coro? It seems that even as they were dying, Vascuna's men had used their remaining strength to bury the gold for safekeeping beneath a tree beside a creek. As John Hemming summed up the expedition:

> *The expedition had lasted over two years and cost the lives of hundreds of Indians and Spaniards. It had failed to find a route to the South Sea [Pacific Ocean], and the excitement over the rich lands beyond the Pacabueyes proved to be a delusion ... An expedition naturally set off the following year taking Francisco Martin to try to locate the tree under which Vascuna's men had buried their gold. It was never found by those or later seekers. It is presumably still there, somewhere between the Catatumbo and Santa Ana Rivers to the west of Lake Maracaibo.*

Ehinger's quest for gold and a golden city had ended in disaster. But the next major expedition into South America would prove far more successful, discovering and then destroying the second of the major Mesoamerican civilizations.

PIZARRO AND THE INCAS

The Spanish had, for some time, heard stories of a vast civilization located somewhere in western South America. Francisco Pizarro, described by Robert Silverberg as "robust, courageous, stubborn, illiterate, cruel, and rapacious," was a veteran explorer who had been with Balboa. He had already traveled as far as the outposts of the Incan Empire and then traveled home to Spain with enough llamas, cloth, silver, and gold in hand to convince Emperor Charles V that a new Mexico was waiting to be conquered.

In July of 1529, Pizarro received the authorization to conquer Peru. Pizarro, who had started out life as a swineherd, was now the governor, captain-general, *adelantado*, and *alguacil-mayor* of Peru for life. All he had to do was return to the New World and conquer the land he had been given.

With just 170 men under his command, Francisco Pizarro marched down the coast of what is today Peru, setting up bases as he went and collecting a goodly amount of gold, silver, and emeralds along the way. It was in some ways a difficult march for, as Robert Silverberg points out, "the tropical sun was fierce on Spanish mail and quilted jackets," but the quest for gold made even the toughest hardships endurable.

Pizarro had followed Cortés's success in Mexico and used what he learned when he took on the Incas. He knew, for example, that the Incas, just like the Aztecs, believed that white-bearded gods would one day appear to them; gods who must be received with respect. He also knew that Incan society, like that of the Aztecs, was built like a pyramid; by removing the man at the top—the emperor—the entire power structure would fall to the Spaniards.

In November of 1532, Pizarro and his men entered the Peruvian town of Cajamarca, where he was soon met by the Incan emperor Atahuallpa, who was brought into town on a litter carried by Incan nobles, all so thoroughly covered with jewelry, that, as one Spaniard wrote, "they blazed like the sun."

Pizarro invited Atahuallpa to become a Christian. Atahuallpa, who thought of himself as a living god, turned down the offer, tossing Pizarro's Bible to the ground. Shots quickly rang out, and within moments, Atahuallpa was a prisoner of the Spanish and Peru and its wealth were now in their hands.

And the wealth was, to say the least, incredible, far exceeding what Cortés had found in Mexico. Francisco Lopez de Gomorra, whose account *Chronica de Indias and Historia de la Conquista de Nueva-Espana*, quoted by Silverberg, was published at Seville in the middle of the seventeenth century, recorded this account of the magnificence that was Atahuallpa.

(The translation is by Sir Walter Raleigh, who will appear later in our story.)

> *All the vessels of his home, table, and kitchen were of gold and silver, and the meanest of silver and copper for strength and hardness of the metal. He had in his wardrobe hollow statues of gold which seemed giants, and the figures in proportion and bigness of all the beasts, birds, trees, and herbs, that the earth bringeth forth: and of all the fishes that the sea or waters of his kingdom breedeth. He had also ropes, budgets, chests and troughs of gold and silver, heaps of billets of gold that seemed wood, marked out to burn.*

An even more astonishing account comes from Garcilaso de la Vegas, the son of a Spanish father and Peruvian mother, who wrote an account of the conquest of Peru sometime around the year 1600. Here, as quoted by Silverberg, he describes the gardens of Atahuallpa's palace:

> *Here were planted the finest trees and the most beautiful flowers and sweet-smelling herbs in the kingdom, while quantities of others were reproduced in gold and silver, at every stage of their growth, from the sprout that hardly shows above the earth, to the full-grown plant, in complete maturity. There were also fields of corn with silver stalks and gold ears, on which the leaves, grains, and even the corn silk were shown. In addition to all this, there were all kinds of gold and silver animals in these gardens, such as rabbits, mice, lizards, snakes, butterflies, foxes, and wildcats (there being no domestic cats). Then there were birds set in the trees as though they were about to sing, and others bent over the flowers, breathing in their nectar. There were row deer and deer, lions and tigers, all the animals in creation, in fact, each placed just where it should be.*
> *Each of these mansions had its bathing suite, with large gold and silver basins into which the water flowed through pipes made of the same metals. And the warm springs in which the Incas went to to bathe were also ornamented with very finely wrought gold trimmings.*

It should be as no surprise that the Spanish felt they'd found the wealth and treasure they'd been looking for; there, hidden away in the

Andes Mountains, was the golden city of their dreams. But what might be a surprise is that to the Incas themselves, the gold was worthless and used just for its value as ornament.

Garcilaso de la Vegas wrote that,

> *Nothing could be bought or sold in their kingdom, where there was neither gold nor silver coin, and these metals could not be considered otherwise than as superfluous, since they could not be eaten, nor could one buy anything to eat with them. Indeed, they were esteemed only for their beauty and brilliance, as being suitable for enhancing that of royal palaces, Sun temples and convents for virgins.*

Indeed, throughout the New World at that time, metal was not used for currency or to pay for things. In Mexico, cacao, the bean that is used to make chocolate, was used as money. In Peru, coca leaves (the source of cocaine) served as currency. So not surprisingly, the Incas were bewildered at the value the Spanish placed on gold but quickly grew to realize that supplying their new rulers with the yellow metal made them very happy.

In fact the deposed emperor Atahuallpa, still being held prisoner by Pizarro, had hopes that with enough gold he could buy his freedom. In exchange for his release, he offered to cover the floor of his cell with gold. Given that his cell measured approximately 25 feet by 17 feet (7.6 meters by 5 meters) in area, the Spaniards reaction to his offer was one of stunned silence. Taking that silence for a rejection, Atahuallpa upped the offer; not only would he supply enough gold to cover the floor of the cell, he'd supply enough gold to cover the floor AND fill it upward as high as he could reach. The offer was accepted, and he was given two months to make good on his offer.

The gold slowly began to come in from all parts of the empire, but the Spanish were not content to sit around and wait. They took over the Incan capital city of Cuzco, home of the Temple of the Sun. That temple, 200 feet (60 m) high, was stripped bare by the gold-hungry Spanish, who tore 700 golden plates from its walls. It is little wonder then that the Spanish, finding golden cities such as Cuzco, were convinced that deep in South America there were more golden cities to be found.

In the meantime, Atahuallpa's ransom had arrived, some of it in the form of golden plates that weighed a remarkable 25 pounds (11 kg) each. The royal fifth was weighted out and sent back to Spain with Pizarro's brother, Hernando. The rest of the gold, treasures of Incan craftsmanship, were melted down, despite the objections of a few who were sorry to see the loss of so many artistic treasures. As Silverberg describes it,

Gold by the weight was what Pizarro's men craved, though, and teams of Indian goldsmiths worked day and night for a full month,

Francisco Pizarro, an experienced explorer, was sent to South America to conquer Peru. As he marched down the coast, gathering riches and establishing Spanish bases, Pizarro met with Incan emperor Atahuallpa. This leader had an elaborate goldsmith workshop in modern-day Quito, Ecuador (*above*).

reducing to uniform yellow ingots the goblets, ewers, and vases, the temple ornaments, the fanciful golden birds and animals, the elegant utensils and cunning artifacts.

It was an extraordinary amount of gold—its value today would be over one billion dollars, the largest ransom in history. But it wasn't enough to satisfy the Spanish. Atahuallpa was put on trial and executed on August 29, 1533, strangled with an iron collar.

As the news of Atahuallpa's death spread throughout the empire, all shipments of gold to the Spanish stopped, and whatever gold was in transit was dumped into the nearest river or lake. Among the items lost, it is said, was a chain of gold 700 feet (213 m) long, weighing several tons. The death of Atahuallpa cost the Spanish more than just lost gold. With their ruler's death, the Incas rose up in revolt against the Spanish, and it took several years of brutal military campaigns before Peru was completely pacified and fully in Spanish hands.

Gold flowed out of Peru at an unbelievable rate. Between 1516 and 1520 Seville recorded receiving 993,000 pesos de oro—the last of the gold from the dwindling West Indian mines and the first to arrive from Panama. Between 1521 and 1525, only 134,000 pesos de oro arrived. The years 1526 to 1530 saw the earliest impact of Cortés's conquering of the Aztec Empire—1,038,000 pesos de oro. But then came the years 1531 to 1535, which reflect the yield from both Mexico and Peru: 1,650,000 pesos de oro. Finally, the years 1536 to 1540 saw the flow at its peak: 3,937,000 pesos de oro arrived in Seville, helping to make Spain the wealthiest nation on the planet.

Those numbers, though, soon began to drop. Grabbing gold from temples and palaces, objects that had been slowly accumulating over time, was one thing. Digging it out of the ground in its raw form was something else again. It soon became apparent that Mexico and Peru would not be enough to sate the Spanish desire and need for gold. The treasuries had been emptied, and the conquered Aztecs and Incas, weakened by disease and resentful of their new masters, showed little interest in helping to dig new mines to enrich the conquistadors.

Fortunately for the Spanish, South America is a large continent: 17,840,000 square kilometers, or 6,890,000 square miles. Spanish conquistadors, all working under royal license and eager to find their own versions of Mexico and Peru, began moving farther down the coast and deeper into the continent, facing uncharted regions, raging rivers, the towering Andes Mountains, steaming tropical rain forests, and tribes both friendly and hostile in their search for gold.

Sebastian de Belalcazar, a lieutenant of Francisco Pizarro, went north into the Andes, toward the Incas' northern capital of Quito (today the capital of Ecuador). The city had been Atahuallpa's base, and rumor had spread that the Incas had plans to make it into a second Cuzco. Surely there'd be great treasures to be found there.

At the same time that de Belalcazar was taking the "easy" route to Quito, advancing along the Andes on a road built by the Incas, Pedro de Alvarado was advancing toward Quito with another expedition, along a route that took them through the lowland forests of Ecuador, north through the jungles of the Macul River, and then through one of the steepest and highest passes of the Andes.

This march to Quito and its hoped-for gold was, in the words of John Hemming,

> ... as cruel as any in the Americas, with a dismal succession of destruction of villages, setting trained dogs on to chiefs or hanging them, and the enslavement of hundreds of innocent lowland Indians.

It also ended in tragedy while, during the march through the Andes, a combination of cold, starvation, and altitude sickness killed 85 European men and women, along with almost all of the Indians that Alvarado had brought with him. Alvarado was forced to admit defeat and sold his equipment to Pizarro, allowing his remaining men to either rejoin Pizarro in Peru or Belalcazar in Quito.

But when they all arrived in Quito in June 1534, they found a town with very little treasure to be had. The area's Incan chiefs, who had fled, were quickly captured and tortured to death or executed in an attempt to get them to reveal where they had hidden the treasures of Atahuallpa. The chiefs, according to contemporary reports, "behaved with great composure and left [Belalcazar] with nothing but his greed. He had them killed inhumanely because he could not rid his mind of his first impression" that there must be treasure to be found.

Indeed, the Spanish were certain that there *was* more treasure to be found. Three separate expeditions, led by Gonzalo Jimenez de Quesada,

Nicholas Federmann, and Sebastian de Belalcazar would all enter the land of the Chibcha Indians, also known as the Muisca, a people renowned for their gold treasures.

And it was from the Muisca and other tribes in the area that stories of a golden kingdom, of a golden king, of a land rich beyond even that of the Incas were heard, and the story and legend of El Dorado was born.

The Lake

Where did the stories come from? Where did they begin? Was there any truth behind the legend? Even the answers to these questions are shrouded in uncertainty.

Timothy Severin, author of *The Golden Antilles*, wrote that just after the collapse of the Incan Empire in 1532, a messenger from an as-yet-unknown tribe appeared in Peru from the northeast. He had come in search of Atahuallpa, and, not having heard that he had been overthrown, walked directly into the hands of the Spanish who, not surprisingly, "persuaded" him to tell them about his mission and about where he had come from.

He told them that he had been sent by the Zipa, a ruling lord of Bogota. He described Bogota as a city rich in gold and other treasures, where a priest-king, covered in gold, would once a year, as part of a religious ceremony, dive into a lake surrounded by high mountains. The story was still in its simplest form, still sketchy and still far from well known, but, as Severin said, "The legend of El Dorado had finally come to the ears of Europeans."

But John Hemming, author of *The Search for El Dorado*, has a slightly different take, dating the story of El Dorado, the golden man, to Quito at the beginning of 1541. It was, in his words,

> *... a beguiling story and it quickly caught the imagination of the conquistadors. It spread fast, gained momentum and credibility, and evolved in detail during the ensuing century. It became one of the*

most famous chimeras [legends] in history, a legend that lured hun-
dreds of hard men into desperate expeditions.

Fernandez de Oviedo, a Spanish explorer and historian of the era, reported the story as he had heard it, careful not to take sides, leaving it to the reader to decide: Truth? Or chimera?

I asked Spaniards who have been in Quito and have come here to
Santo Domingo ... why they call that prince the "Golden Chief or
King." They tell me that what they have learned from the Indians is
that the great lord or prince goes about continually covered in gold
dust as fine as ground salt. He feels that it would be less beautiful to
wear any other ornament. It would be crude and less common to put
on armour plates of hammered or stamped gold, for other rich lords
wear these when they wish. But to powder oneself with gold is some-
thing exotic, unusual, novel and more costly—for he washes away at
night what he puts on each morning, so that is discarded and lost,
and he does this every day of the year.

Oviedo, naturally, was astonished at the thought of a land that had so much gold that it would waste it in such a way:

I would rather have the sweepings of the chamber of this prince
than the great meltings of gold there have been in Peru or that there
could be anywhere on earth! For the Indians say that this chief or
king is a very rich and great ruler. He anoints himself every morn-
ing with a certain gum or resin that sticks very well. The powdered
gold adheres to that unction ... until his entire body is covered
from the soles of his feet to his head. He looks as resplendent as a
gold object worked by the hand of a great artist. I believe that, if
that chief does do this, he must have very rich mines of fine quality
gold.

Oviedo wrote his account with a slightly skeptical, but still open mind, telling it as it was told to him, while at the same time warning that it was based on hearsay from Indian sources. The story that he told, while seemingly highly unlikely, was not utterly impossible to believe,

The legend of El Dorado can be traced to a story about a prince who painted himself in gold dust. As the story spread from person to person, different versions of it began appearing in published accounts of famous explorers. *Above*, an engraving from Sir Walter Raleigh's book depicts natives spraying gold on a nobleman.

especially when the wealth of the area and in previously discovered areas was taken into account.

It was, in fact, a tradition for the inhabitants of that area to paint their bodies for special occasions. On the other hand, a Jesuit priest named José Gumilla who lived with the indigenous inhabitants of the Orinoco Valley in South America noted that daily anointments were done as well, as found in Norma Gaffron's *El Dorado, Land of Gold*:

> *With very few exceptions, all tribes of those lands anoint themselves from the crowns of their heads to the tips of their feet with oil and*

achiote. Mothers anoint all their children, even those at the breast, at the same time as they anoint themselves, at least twice a day in the morning and at nightfall. They later anoint their husbands very liberally. On special days a great variety of drawings in different colours goes on top of the unction ... The ordinary daily unction is a mixture of oil and annatto that we call achiote. It is ground and kneaded with oil of cundama or turtle eggs. It serves not only as clothing but as a sure defence against mosquitoes, which abound in such a great number of species. It not only prevents mosquitoes from biting them, but the insects stick in the gum.

John Hemming adds to this, noting that not only does the anointment serve to cool the skin and protect it from the sun, but that to this day tribes in the Amazon still do this regularly, painting their skin with scarlet annatto and black genipapo vegetable dyes. All of which raises two questions: If the indigenous people were painting themselves red or black, is it possible that some painted themselves gold as well? Or ... is it also possible over the course of time and storytelling, the original sightings of tribes in their red and black colors were transformed to stories of golden men?

WAS THERE A LAKE?

The story of a golden land began to appear in other chronicles as well. Pedro de Cieza de León, a soldier and historian who wrote an account of the conquest of Peru, was the only contemporary author to actually visit Quito, in the late 1540s. He wrote that Gonzalo Pizarro, the youngest brother of Francisco, had gone to Quito in 1521, and, as cited by John Hemming, "observing in that city many [unemployed] men, either youths or veterans, he became eager to discover the valley of El Dorado."

This valley, according to the stories, was located somewhere beyond the mountains east of Quito. In fact, an expedition had just returned from an attempt to find cinnamon (a much-valued spice) in that same area, the territory of the Quijos Indians.

The Indians said that further on, if they advanced, they would come to a wide-spreading flat country, teeming with Indians who possess great riches, for they all wear gold ornaments, and where there are no forests or mountain ranges. When this news spread in Quito, everyone there wanted to take part in the expedition.

Gonzalo Pizarro himself was so excited by the news that he wrote to the King that,

... because of many reports which I received in Quito and outside that city, from prominent and very aged chiefs as well as from Spaniards, whose accounts agreed with one another, that the province of La Canela [Cinnamon] and Lake El Dorado were a very populous and very rich land, I decided to go and conquer and explore it.

According to John Hemming, this is the first time that the legend of El Dorado was linked to a lake.

Once El Dorado was said to be located by a lake, stories of sacrifice by a lake quickly circulated, started by Juan de Castellanos, the vicar of Tunja, a writer whose histories were closer to epic poetry than fact-based history. He wrote about what he had learned from the Spanish general Gonzalo Jimenez de Quesada, who had explored the land of the Muisca and had written about the lakes in which they threw in their gold and precious stones as a religious sacrifice, as well as from Sebastian de Belalcazar:

Belalcazar interrogated a foreign, itinerant Indian resident in the city of Quito, who said he was a citizen of Bogota and had come there by I know not what means. He stated that [Bogota] was a land rich in emeralds and gold. Among the things that attracted them, he told of a certain king, unclothed, who went on rafts on a pool to make oblations, which he had observed, anointing all [his body] with resin and on top of it a quantity of ground gold, from the bottom of his feet to his forehead, gleaming like a ray of the sun. He also said that there was continual traffic there to make offerings of gold jewellery, fine emeralds, and other pieces of their ornaments ... The soldiers, delighted and content, then gave [that king] the name El Dorado; and they spread out [in search of him] by innumerable routes.

As John Hemming stated, it is these authors—Fernandez de Oviedo, Pedro de Cieza de León, and Juan de Castellanos, as well as the conquistadores Gonzalo Pizarro, Gonzalo Jimenez de Quesada, and Sebastian de Belalcazar, who are the primary sources for the legend of El Dorado. Every other writer simply elaborated and embellished on these early accounts.

It would fall to Father Pedro Simon to turn the early accounts of El Dorado into legend. His book *Noticias historiales de las conquistas*, written in 1621–1623, borrowed liberally (some would say shamelessly plagiarized) from Castellanos's account, turning his poetry into prose and adding details that, to Father Simon at least, made sense.

He wrote that the Indian called his homeland Musequeta and its chief Bogota, and he added a description of the raft, lake, and gold dust ceremony that he claimed took place on a crystal-clear morning with the

When Gonzalo Pizarro found out from local chiefs that there was a large city of gold by a lake, he believed they were describing the city of El Dorado. People began to publish false accounts of the city, including Father Pedro Simon, who claimed that Lake El Dorado was in fact Lake Guatavita (*above*) in modern-day Colombia.

sun's rays perfectly illuminating the golden chief. Father Simon went on to link this account with the Muisca custom (as previously described by Belalcazar) of making sacrifices to lakes. He stated categorically that the ceremony took place at Lake Guatavita, a round lake located in the hills 50 kilometers (31 miles) northeast of Bogota.

(Simon also added to the legend by adding the story of the unfaithful wife of a chief of Guatavita, who, not able to cope with her husband's contempt, threw herself and her daughter into the lake. There she remained, living with a monster, which led to visions of the chieftainess, which led in turn to a cult being formed around her, with offerings being thrown into the lake to earn her protection. Simon said that the chief himself then started to gild his body, to absorb into himself his own offerings, and when the Spanish invaded the area, the Indians threw all of their treasures into the sacred lake.)

The story changed even more with its next telling, by Juan Rodriguez Fresle (also known as Freyle), in his 1636 book, *Conquest and Discovery of New Granada*. In his telling, the gilding ceremony was now the age-old ritual of the investiture of the successor to the Zipa of Bogota. The heir would have his Muisca cloaks removed, be anointed with gum and gold dust, and then be launched out onto the lake along with four other chiefs and a sizable mound of gold and emeralds. As the ceremony, with its accompanying chanting and music reached its peak, the chief-to-be and his court would then throw their gold and emeralds into the lake as tribute. As Fresle wrote, "From this ceremony was taken that famous name 'El Dorado' that has cost so many lives and fortunes . . . "

There were other stories as well, including one by the eighteenth-century author Basilio Vicente de Oviedo, which described El Dorado as being a land so rich with gold that tufts of grass pulled out of the ground had gold dust clinging to their roots! He also told of a yearly event where a young man was chosen by lot and offered as a sacrifice to their idol. "They open him up and salt him with gold dust, and offer him as a sacrifice in their church. Because of this they call him El Dorado." Could any of these stories really be true?

THE TRUTH BEHIND THE LEGEND

As we have seen, the legend of El Dorado changed over time from a shadowy idea of a rich, flat land east of Quito, to Fernandez de Oveido's prince anointed daily with gold, to the offerings of Juan de Castellanos, to the chief with the wayward wife of Father Simon, to the investiture ceremonies of Juan Rodriguez Fresle, to the sacrifice of Basilio de Oviedo.

With each recounting the story grew more elaborate and more detailed. But what is it that all these stories have in common? There's an Indian messenger who arrives at Quito. There's a lake. There's the anointment with gold dust. Let's examine each of these elements and find the truth behind the stories.

Is it possible, as the stories said, that the Indian messenger, the "indio dorado" captured near Quito was in fact a messenger from the Muisca? Highly unlikely. Before the arrival of the Spanish, the Incas had controlled a large area around Quito, and the Muisca at that time were under no threat that would have required sending a single messenger on a long and perilous journey to Quito. In addition, no conquistador ever found any sign of trade or even contact between the Muisca and the Incas!

Is it possible that El Dorado was a lake? After all, Gonzalo Pizarro wrote to the king in 1542 that he was searching for "Lake El Dorado." But there is no other early source that connects El Dorado with a lake. And while it is true that the Muisca did venerate lakes, their main focus of worship was up above: the sun, the moon, and the stars.

And while it's true that some Muisca artifacts have been found in the beds of old lakes, those finds have been few and far between, not nearly enough to back up the stories of gold and precious stones being poured into the water during religious and investiture ceremonies.

But perhaps even more important, the Muisca themselves did not produce gold. They obtained it by trading with other tribes, and the items they crafted from that gold tended to be small and relatively insignificant, and definitely not enough to have allowed them to waste the amount of gold that is described in the El Dorado legends. So, while there was some religious significance given to Lake Guatavita, it was not in any way central to Muisca beliefs and could not have been the source of the powerful legend of El Dorado.

The story of gold dust, as well, is questionable. Sebastian de Belalcazar claimed to have found Indians, in the Neiva region of the upper Magdalena, in possession of gold dust. Pedro de Puelles as well, had traveled down the Magdalena and testified on his return about the "fine gold and

EL DORADO IN POPULAR CULTURE

The words *El Dorado* have become part of our cultural heritage. Books, songs, automobiles, animated films, even brands of rum have used the words to bring to mind images of gold and treasure, of something valuable just within one's grasp. One of the most memorable uses of the theme of El Dorado was in the poem of the same name by Edgar Allan Poe (January 19, 1809–October 7, 1849), an American author perhaps best known for his short stories.

ELDORADO

Gaily bedight,
 A gallant knight,
 In sunshine and in shadow,
  Had journeyed long,
  Singing a song,
 In search of Eldorado.

But he grew old—
 This knight so bold—
 And o'er his heart a shadow
  Fell as he found
  No spot of ground
 That looked like Eldorado.

And, as his strength
 Failed him at length,
 He met a pilgrim shadow—
  "Shadow," said he,
  "Where can it be—
 This land of Eldorado?"

"Over the Mountains
 Of the Moon,
 Down the Valley of the Shadow,
  Ride, boldly ride,"
  The shade replied—
 "If you seek for Eldorado!"

gold dust from mines" that could be found in the reaches of the upper Magdalena. He also hinted that there was more to be found.

But according to John Hemming, the very idea of gold dust so fine that it would be used like powder to anoint (like the dyes used by the Orinoco Indians) seems to have become mixed into earlier beliefs that the richest areas, the best sources of gold, could be found closest to the equator, where the weather was hottest. It was in these areas where anointing with dyes to keep cool was the most prevalent.

The legend of El Dorado then, according to all contemporary sources, started in Quito and began to take form in late 1540. The story apparently originated not from an "itinerant Indian messenger" but from the Spaniards themselves, returning *from* Bogota. Explorers Gonzalo Jimenez de Quesada, Nicholas Federmann, and Sebastian de Belalcazar, in their journeys, had seen enough and heard enough to encourage their belief that, located somewhere deep in the area, was a city of gold.

They didn't call it El Dorado—they didn't know it by such a name and would not, in fact, refer to it as such. But now that we know how the legend of El Dorado was created by the chroniclers of the period writing about Quesada, Federmann, and Belalcazar, in our next chapter we will go back several years, to the journeys they made that inspired the chronicles, and then from there we will go *forward* to the journeys inspired *by* the chronicles.

The Obsession Begins

Elegias de Varones Illustres de Indias was written by Juan de Castellanos in 1589, many years after the events he recounts. It purports to tell the story of how an Indian messenger arrived in Quito with tales of a golden Indian "El Dorado," whose kingdom was still to be discovered. Whether this account is true is questionable, as we have seen. But what is known for certain is that shortly after his march into Quito, Sebastian de Belalcazar went back out on another expedition.

Surprisingly, if Castellanos's chronicle was correct and Belalcazar knew about the "gilded man" named El Dorado, his mission was not to find gold. His goal, as quoted by Hemming, was "to discover what lay between Quito and the North Sea [Caribbean]." Leaving his lieutenant in charge of Quito, Belalcazar set off on his expedition, along with several giant mastiff dogs, cattle, horses, hundreds of Indian bearers, and a huge herd of swine and pregnant sows. According to Victor von Hagen, "Progress was thus pig-paced."

But progress was made. Although there had been occasional return trips to Quito to protect himself from political foes among the Spanish, by 1537 Belalcazar had founded the cities of Popayan and Cali. In July of 1538, Belalcazar, along with 200 of his men, discovered the source of the upper Magdalena River. And finally, later that year, they reached the land of the Muisca Indians on the plateau of Bogota. Still dressed in their finery, in their rich clothes of silk and coats of mail, they were shocked to learn that they were not the only Spanish in the area. Another group had gotten there first.

Sebastian de Belalcazar organized a large crew for an exploratory expedition from Quito to the Caribbean. Along the way, Belalcazar established two cities but soon found out that he was not the only European explorer in the area.

ANOTHER EXPEDITION JOINS THE SEARCH

In 1536, Gonzalo Jimenez de Quesada had begun exploring to the south of Santa Marta on Colombia's northern coast with a well-organized expedition of somewhere between 500 and 800 men. The journey started badly; the land beginning at Santa Marta and going for nearly 150 miles (241 km) inland was barren of both water and gold. In addition, the men found themselves under constant guerilla-style attacks by the Chimela Caribs, armed with the one weapon that truly frightened the well-armed Spaniards: poison arrows. There was no cure; anyone seriously wounded by a poisoned arrow would be dead within days. Chronicler Pedro de Aguado wrote that if the arrow drew blood,

> *... the poison flows along the bloodstream and reaches the heart within twenty-four hours, where the herbal poison reigns with greater force. It causes trembling and convulsions of the body, and loss of reason that makes men say bold, terrible things of such dubious faith for dying men. In the end they die in such a desperate state that the living are often prompted to kill them themselves rather than await such a death.*

There was also disease to contend with, as well as snakes and alligators, and a hostile climate and geography. Quesada and his men pushed on though, until the climate and landscape suddenly changed. They were now up on a fertile plateau 8,200–9,200 feet (2,500–2,804 m) above sea level, where corn, beans, and nuts were being grown. They were in the land of the Muisca.

It was a land of cultivated farms, filled with crops that were entirely new to the Spanish: potatoes and corn, squash and chili peppers, pineapples and avocados. It was a land of plenty, a land that was largely disease-free, and a land where the Spaniards always had enough to eat. As Fernandez de Oviedo wrote:

> *... it was noteworthy that during the two years of that conquest, there was not a single day when food of [all] local varieties failed to arrive in the Spaniards' camp in great abundance. There were days of a hundred or 150 deer, and at the very least thirty deer in a day.*

And a conquest it was, albeit, at least at the beginning, a peaceful one. The reception from the Muisca to the Spanish was friendly; gifts of gold, emeralds, and food were readily given by the locals, awestruck by the Spanish costumes, horses, weaponry, and sheer foreignness. Quesada did his best to help preserve the peace by issuing orders that there should be no looting or abuse of the Indians by any Spaniard. To make his point clear, one soldier, known to history as Juan Gordo ("Fat John") was ordered hanged for stealing a poncho from a Muisca.

The peace, however, didn't last long. The Zipa of Bogota massed his troops to repel the Spanish invaders from his land. The Muisca attacked on March 22, 1537, carrying the mummified body of the previous Bogota

GOLD OR POTATOES?

Potatoes, which originated in southern Peru and were first domesticated between 3000 and 2000 B.C., were the main source of energy for the Incan Empire, its predecessors, and its Spanish successor.

According to legend, when the mythical founders of the Incan Empire, Manco Capac and Mama Ocillo, emerged from the waters of Lake Titicaca, the first thing the god Wiracocha taught them was how to sow potatoes. Possibly due to this honorable origin, the farmers of the Andes have managed to create a series of varieties that have adapted to a wide range of climates within Peru itself.

In fact, as hard as it may be to believe, more than 3,000 varieties of potato are grown in Peru! They come in a variety of colors: pink, white, blue, purple, yellow, or brown. They come in a wide range of sizes and shapes: Some are round, some are shaped like fingers, some are as small as grapes, some are as big as your fist. The textures and flavors vary just as dramatically: from starchy to waxy, and from nutty to bitter to sweet.

And here's something even more difficult to believe. The potato, as humble as it may appear, was by far the greatest treasure found in the Andes. In fact, if you add up the value of the world's annual potato harvest, it is worth many times over the value of *all* the precious metals looted from the Muisca and Incan empires!

and other heroes in litters at their head. But they were no match for the Spanish conquistadors and their horses, the largest animals seen in South America.

The Spanish had sizable advantages other than their fearsome horses. The Muisca went up against the heavily armored and armed invaders with nothing more than sharp wooden swords, javelins, and wooden shields. They had no bows and arrows. They had no curare or other poisons. Belalcazar, as cited by Hemming, referred to them as "very spineless, cowardly and feminine people, badly armed and without poison."

The battle was a defeat for the Muisca. Days later, Quesada and his men marched triumphantly into the valley of Bogota, the heart of the Muisca homeland and the seat of government for its most powerful ruler. There, "they began to see beautiful and magnificent buildings, houses and palaces of wood, more ornate and better than all they had seen before." They moved through the valley, trying to make alliances and fighting constant skirmishes as they went, until sometime around April 21, 1537, they arrived at the palace of Muequeta, the residence of the king they had come to conquer.

The conquest of the Muisca homelands, despite all the Spaniards' advantages, took more than a year to complete. By the time it was all over, each of the rulers of the area had been defeated and their treasures ransacked. From the chambers of the Zaque of Tunja alone, enough treasure was seized to make a pile the height of a mounted horseman: 136,500 pesos (61 kilos) of fine gold, 14,000 pesos of base gold, and 280 emeralds.

The treasures were of amazing workmanship, based on what little has survived; the Muisca goldsmiths were capable of producing masterpieces. The Muisca, though, had no source of gold of their own. What gold they had, they had obtained through trade, largely salt and cotton cloth. The Spanish grabbed whatever gold was readily and easily available, from temples, tombs (despite any moral objections to desecrating burial sites), and wherever else it could be found.

By June of 1538 the time had finally come: the melting down of the amassed treasure, to be divided among all the members of the expedition. The amounts depended on rank. The treasure was divided into 289 "parts." At the top of the ranking, the governor of Santa Marta was assigned 10 parts, Quesada, 9 parts. At the bottom of the pyramid was the ordinary swordsman or soldier, who received one part.

Gonzalo Jimenez de Quesada and his crew headed inland from Colombia's northern coast and managed to push through rough terrain and bad weather to reach the land of the Muiscas. While the group did not have direct access to gold, the Muiscas were adept at working with the metal and used it to create beautiful items. *Above,* a gold Muisca dragon.

So how much did that work out to for two years of effort? Each "part" was calculated (the records of this transaction still survive) at 510 pesos (2.320 kilos) of fine gold, 57 pesos (260 grams) of base gold, and five emeralds—in today's figures, well over $500,000 per "part." This, then, was the reward for being one of the tiny number of brave adventurers who made their way into the South American wilderness.

And amazingly, at the same time that Belalcazar was moving into Colombia from the south, and Quesada was moving in from Santa Marta on the coast, another group of conquistadors was entering into Colombia's eastern region. The Welsers of Germany had not given up on South America and had replaced the dead Ambrosius Ehinger with Georg Hohermuth as Venezuela's new governor. Hohermuth set out in May of 1535 from

Coro with 400 men and 80 horses, on what was planned as a great two-and-a-half-year expedition in search of gold and treasure.

They returned nearly three years later, in failure. As John Hemming explains it, going out in search of treasure was similar to a game of blind man's bluff. Hohermuth, in the course of his expedition, had "blundered past great riches—the land of the Muisca—and hurried off into oblivion." With no maps available to explore unknown territory, dependent on Indian guides with little interest in helping the conquistadors, the men wandered through the wilderness, slowly being killed off by heat, disease, and Indian attacks before the survivors managed to make their way back to Coro. As one of the men, Philip von Hutten, described their decision to give up and try to get back to Coro, ". . . we turn back, suffering as much misery and privation as, in my opinion, any Christians had ever previously suffered."

At the same time that Hohermuth's expedition was headed for failure, his lieutenant, Nicholas Federmann, was heading an expedition of his own, following up on Ehinger's exploration beyond Maracaibo. His journey, which also began with high hopes, quickly began to fall apart the farther they moved inland from Coro, as quoted from a firsthand report:

> Some soldiers whom thirst tormented most, went off to seek water. They plunged inland into the interior, which was very flat in some parts of that land. They easily became foolish: they lost their direction and could never again strike the path along which they had entered. They marched like madmen from place to place, until overcome by exhaustion and lack of strength they could no longer move from one side to the other, and they remained there, wherever this sad siren had summoned them, self-important, and dead.

Not only was there a lack of food and water, when the expedition finally made its way to the land of the Pacabueyes, they found that there was no more gold left in the province; what gold there had been was thoroughly swept clean by Ehinger and by men from Santa Marta. Federmann left the majority of his surviving men in the hills of Carora to establish a base and returned to Coro in September 1536. Once there, hearing tales that the province of Meta was where gold was to be found in abundance, he set out once again, picking up his men along the way to the mountains, where, for the next two years, he spent a futile search for a kingdom of gold.

THE MEETING

After Quesada had completed the conquest of the Muisca and their gold had been distributed, he began to plan his next move. Within just twenty years, the kingdoms of the Aztec, the Inca, and the Muisca had been conquered and pillaged by the Spanish, resulting in the greatest discovery of gold, silver, and jewels in the history of mankind. Surely, in a land of such wonders and treasures, there was more gold to be had even farther into the interior. Interesting stories were beginning to be heard, of golden men and golden kingdoms, deeper in the South American heartland.

Other stories were being heard by Quesada as well. Word came from Indians from the land of a Mosca chief called Pasca that there were other Christians in the valley, and they drew pictures of the horses and pigs they had seen. Men were sent to investigate and found that, indeed, there were other Christians in the valley. Sebastian de Belalcazar and his men, who had been making expeditions out of Quito since 1536, had arrived.

The meeting between the two groups was, understandably, rather wary. Belalcazar and his men were still dressed in their finest garb, while, as von Hagen wrote, "years in battle and terrifying travels had reduced Quesada's men to appear as mounted gypsies." Yet, those mounted gypsies had defeated the Muisca and were concerned about whether they would be able to maintain their control against Belalcazar's better-armed expedition.

More bad news soon arrived, as quoted by John Hemming in his book *The Search for El Dorado*:

> We learned that, from the direction of the plains to which we had been unable to emerge—which is towards the sun rise—other Christians were coming, and that there were many of them, with many horses! We were considerably amazed by this and could not think who it could be.

The new group was based only six leagues away, in the lands of Pasca. It turned out to be, of course, the remaining members of Nicholas Federmann's expedition from Venezuela. Against all odds, three expeditions in search of lands and treasure had all converged, in February of 1539, in a triangle in the homeland of the Muisca.

It was a legendary meeting. Quesada's officers exclaimed, as quoted by Hemming, "We considered it a great marvel for men from three governorships—from Peru and Venezuela and Santa Marta—to join up in a place so remote from the sea." But Quesada was in a tricky position. Each of the other expeditions was better armed than his, each had endured considerable hardships just to reach Bogota, each was led by an ambitious lieutenant governor, and each believed, based on geography, that the lands of the Muisca lay within their own governor's control.

Quesada, a trained lawyer, quickly reached agreements with the two other leaders. Federmann would receive 40 pounds of gold and emeralds taken from the Muisca in exchange for equipment and livestock. His men would be allowed to remain as colonists. A similar deal was reached with Belalcazar. And, it was decided, that the three men would travel together to Spain, to present their cases to the king and the Council of the Indies, and allow *them* to decide how the Muisca lands should be divided.

Each man ended up being disappointed. Nicholas Federmann ended up fighting with the Welser Company and died in February 1542. Quesada returned to Spain with hundreds of emeralds along with promises of gold to come for his king but ended up facing lawsuit after lawsuit by members of his expedition who had been left behind along the way but still wanted their share of the treasure. He eventually fled to France. Belalcazar, the conqueror of Quito, was made governor not of Bogota as he wanted, but of Popayan and made plans for further expeditions.

Despite the disappointing end to their personal stories, the tales of the gold they had discovered and of the wonders they had seen quickly spread throughout South America and Spain. And along with those tales were stories about things they hadn't yet seen, tales of even richer kingdoms of gold, of golden kingdoms and golden kings. Their stories, as incredible as they were in reality, inspired even more incredible stories—the stories of a land that came to be known as El Dorado.

The Amazon

By 1541, the legend of El Dorado was firmly in the mind of many a Spanish conquistador eager to make his fortune. As John Hemming wrote:

> El Dorado [was responsible for sending] men marching into the depths of South America. And their target area was the eastern foothills of the Andes [372 miles] southwest of Bogota—one of the wildest places in all the rough interior of South America.

It took a certain kind of foolhardy bravery to make the journey. The climate was unforgiving. The terrain was treacherous, supplies were limited, maps were nonexistent, and the explorers faced a continuous threat from the people already inhabiting the land who, not surprisingly, did not always look kindly on Spanish explorers coming in, stealing their gold, attempting to convert them to Catholicism, making them into slaves, or even killing them in the process. But to the explorers, the lure of riches and fame overpowered any risks.

Fifteen forty-one became another year of expeditions, and the first major one to set out was led by Gonazlo Pizarro, brother of Francisco Pizarro, the conqueror of the Incas. Gonzalo had become governor of Quito on December 1, 1540, and within a matter of weeks after taking office, he had decided to leave Quito and set out in search of El Dorado and the land of Cinnamon.

Land of Cinnamon? It's important to remember that while gold was definitely a priority for anyone heading out into the South American jungle, there were other things being sought after as well, and one of them was cinnamon. It was popular throughout Europe for its flavor, and for the fact that its flavor could be used to mask the taste of rotting meat in the days before refrigeration. When the Pizarros conquered Peru, they noted the Incas seemed to have a source for cinnamon, a source they were determined to find.

In February 1541, Gonzalo Pizarro left Quito with 220 Spanish adventurers assisted by the forced labor of more than 4,000 Indian porters, along with crossbows, firearms, almost 200 horses, llamas, more than a thousand live hogs, and hunting dogs that had also been trained to attack Indians. As they set out, Hemming noted, "Each man carried only a sword and a shield, with a small sack of food beneath it." Everything else was carried by the llamas and the Indian porters.

Pizarro is described by Hemming as being the picture of a conquistador: "brave, handsome, magnificently dressed when the occasion was appropriate, a fine horseman and swordsman, but, according to his cousin, rather mean." Expecting to find well-built Incan roads going east out of Quito, the expedition found only hard going, first crossing high mountain ranges where many of the Indians died of cold, before plunging into steamy jungles, where it was necessary for those in the lead to use machetes to cut a path for the horses.

Just thirty leagues from Quito (a little over 100 miles [160 km]), Pizarro was forced to order a rest because "both the Spaniards and the horses were all quite exhausted from the great hardships which they had endured . . ." No mention was made in the report of the hardships the local porters had endured.

They began to find some cinnamon trees, but they were scattered throughout the dense, lightly populated landscape, and it quickly became apparent that it would not be possible to farm them commercially. Pizarro was not happy with this turn of events, and when the local population was unable to tell him where he might find richer areas worth exploring, he refused to take them at their word. Hemming cited this account by Cieza de León:

Gonzalo Pizarro was angry that the Indians had given no reply in conformity with what he wanted. He went on to ask them other questions, but they always answered in the negative.

Pizarro refused to accept their answers, and ordered cane platforms to be built:

> ... and the Indians to be put on them and tortured until they told the truth. The innocent natives were promptly stretched on those frames or barbecues by the cruel Spaniards, and some of them were burned ... The butcher Gonzalo Pizarro, not content with burning Indians who had committed no fault, further ordered that other Indians should be thrown to the dogs, who tore them to pieces with their teeth and devoured them. I heard that there were some women among those who were burned or eaten in this way, which made it worse.

Pizarro found himself stuck in the jungle hills, plagued by heavy rains and running desperately short on food. Pizarro set out ahead on foot, along with 80 other men, leaving the horses and the others at Zumaco under his second in command, Francisco de Orellana. They headed out into what was truly the unknown, hacking their way forward through what seemed like endless forests, never knowing what was ahead, trying desperately to find streams and water. It was exhausting, backbreaking work. Hemming noted:

> By the end of a few weeks of such toil, men are pale and thin, with their clothes torn and boots disintegrating. Their skin is covered in bites, thorns, and festering scratches; and the glands that filter insect poison from the arms and legs are sore and swollen. Gonzalo Pizarro's men were moving in the wet season, when the forest is dripping with rain, there is danger from falling trees and branches, and the ground rapidly turns to slimy pink mud, or swamp, or flooding. This is the season when mosquitoes are most active.

Things continued to get worse as flash floods washed away most of the expedition's remaining supplies. Pizarro himself "frequently deplored having undertaken this expedition." Upon finally reaching a broad river, probably the Napo, the ragged forces were inspected by a local chief called Delicola, who wanted to see for himself what kind of men had invaded his territory. When he learned of the atrocities the Spanish had inflicted on other tribes, Delicola did what he could to get rid of them, telling him that farther on there were "very rich regions full of powerful lords."

Those were just the words that Pizarro and his men wanted to hear. The expedition reunited at Zumaco, smaller expeditions were sent out, and captives were interrogated and tortured in the hopes of getting additional information, but nothing was accomplished. Month after month passed, with nothing to show for it. At one point, Pizarro was convinced that he had received real hard news of the rich lands he was seeking, but instead of locating the El Dorado of his dreams, all he found was another marshy province.

The expedition pushed on, finally reaching the banks of a broad river, possibly the Coca, which is one of the main sources of the Napo, itself a tributary to the mighty Amazon River. It seems likely that while Pizarro and his men knew that these rivers to the east of the Andes flowed out into the Atlantic, they had no concept of how long the journey was and how large the continent was, and no concept whatsoever of the sheer size of the Amazon.

They did, though, come to the decision that their best option would be to build a raft that could carry their remaining supplies downriver, while the horses followed along on land, doing so, as Pizarro wrote, "in the hope of reaching some region of plenty, for which they all besought Our Lord." Pizarro was determined that if such a region could not be found, they would stay on the river until it reached the Atlantic. His second in command, Francisco de Orellana, was equally determined that the expedition should continue the search for treasure overland.

The boat was built, and for 43 days the expedition slowly made its way downstream. Supplies began to run out, and the men were slowly starving to death. As one of the four captured Indian chiefs made his escape, he told his captors that there was a rich and prosperous country to be found up a river to the east. Pizarro, desperate to save his men, allowed Orellana to take the boat, along with 60 men, and go out in search of food and supplies. He never returned.

Instead of finding food, Orellana and his men worked their way down the entire length of the Amazon to the Atlantic, leaving Gonzalo Pizarro and his men to make their way back overland to Quito. Was it treachery on Orellana's part? Orellana claimed that the currents were too strong to allow him to make it back. Pizarro, on the other hand, was convinced that Orellana's behavior was treacherous, as cited in Hemming:

> *Being confident that Captain Orellana would do as he said, because he was my lieutenant, I told him that I was pleased at the idea of his going for food . . . and gave him the brig and sixty men . . . But instead of bringing food, he went down the river without leaving any arrangements . . . He thus displayed towards the whole expedition the greatest cruelty that faithless men have ever shown. He was aware that it was left unprovided with food, trapped in a vast uninhabited region and among great rivers.*

Trapped in unknown forests, rained on day and night, Pizarro and his men tried to survive while waiting for Orellana to return, unaware that he was moving farther and farther toward the Atlantic. They were forced to eat the remaining horses and dogs. Finally, Pizarro sent men out to search for either Orellana or food; they managed to stumble across an abandoned Indian manioc plantation.

Manioc (also known as yucca or cassava) has an edible starchy root. Two full canoes of manioc root were loaded and brought back to Pizarro and his men. They had been waiting there for 27 days and had been reduced to eating their saddles and stirrup leathers; they had begun to give up all hope that they would be able to survive.

The entire expedition moved back to the manioc plantation before setting back out through the jungle, hoping to find their way back to Quito. Suffering from diarrhea from eating nothing but manioc they set out, "nearly dead with hunger, naked and barefoot, covered with sores, opening the path with their swords. Meanwhile, it rained, so that on many days they never saw the sun and could not get dry."

Finally, after months of the most harrowing and arduous journey imaginable, they saw a line of mountains in the east. The survivors, only one-quarter of the men who had originally been left behind by Orellana, arrived in Quito in June 1542, nearly a year and a half after they had left in a glorious display of Spanish strength, each man with nothing more than his sword and his staff in his hand.

The expedition had been a spectacular failure. When rival conquistador Sebastian de Belalcazar wrote to the king describing his failure in the Land of Cinnamon (Belalcazar still wanted to find El Dorado himself), Gonzalo Pizarro returned to Bolivia to live off the wealth he had amassed while helping his brother conquer the Inca Empire. But when the Spanish government issued the "New Laws" for the governance of the Americas that the Spanish settlers felt were too lenient toward the natives, the settlers rebelled and summoned Pizarro to lead them in a revolt against Spain.

For four years, Pizarro and his men ruled Peru in a brutal dictatorship, compounding the Indians' anguish. Spain, in an attempt to end the conflict, revoked the pro-Indian laws and sent forces in to squash the rebels. After many battles, Gonzalo Pizarro, the first man to set out specifically in search for El Dorado, was defeated and hanged outside the former Inca capital of Cuzco in 1548.

Meanwhile, while Pizarro and his men were still struggling to return to Quito, Orellana and his men were making history on their way down the Amazon. As their journey down the Napo in search of food began, Orellana and his men were in very bad shape. Food supplies were so low that they were soon reduced to eating animal hides and the soles of their shoes boiled and cooked with herbs. Many of them were too weak to even stand and were so desperate for food that they would crawl into the forest in search of food and ended up eating poisonous roots. Seven men died of starvation the first week alone.

According to Orellana's later account, they were in fact ready to give up and return to the main force waiting with Pizarro, but the currents were simply too strong. They had no choice but to keep going, until they finally came upon a tribe of prosperous Indians, who being told by Orellana that they were sons of the sun, were more than happy to share their food. They stayed there for a month, expecting that Pizarro might follow. He didn't of course, and, anxious to go forward and test the idea that the river would flow into the Atlantic, they built a second, sturdier boat and set sail, not in search of El Dorado any longer, but on a voyage of pure discovery.

What none of them knew (or even suspected) was that they were the first Europeans to attempt to travel down the Amazon, the world's largest river. By any standard—its breadth and depth, the size of its basin, and the sheer volume of water that flows down it to the Atlantic (one-fifth of all the freshwater that flows into the ocean comes from the Amazon)—it completely dwarfs the competition.

Spanish settlers and conquistadors became angry when Emperor Charles V passed laws that prevented the exploitation of native peoples in South America. The settlers recruited Gonzalo Pizarro to help them rebel against the crown, but royal forces ended the rebellion and publicly executed Pizarro (*above*).

Orellana and his 50 surviving men began descending down the Napo toward the Maranon and Amazon. For the many tribes living in small villages along the river's bank, they were the first white men they had ever seen. It was, to say the least, a shock; some reacted in terror, running away to hide in the forests, allowing the Spanish free reign to take the food from their village. Others turned out to greet the strange men in their full tribal regalia.

Once they reached the main stream of the Amazon, members of the powerful Machiparo branch of the Omagua nation rowed out in canoes to inform the Spanish that their chief wanted to meet them. Orellana and his men entered the village with weapons ready, but when the chief gave them a warm welcome and offered the strangers part of the village to occupy, they lowered their weapons and defenses.

Unfortunately, seeing that there was plenty of food available, including maize, yams, peanuts, turtles, and fish, they also ran amok and started grabbing all the food they could put their starving hands on. Their hosts rightly concluded that these were not bearded gods but simply hungry, greedy men, so they attacked, coming at the Spaniards with clubs and spears, while protected by shields of crocodile or manatee skin. Sixteen Spanish were wounded and two were killed before they managed to get organized and fight back against their attackers.

Farther downstream were the villages of the great Omagua tribe, which the Spanish praised for their "numerous and very large settlements and very pretty country and very fruitful land." Not only was the land beautiful, the Omagua were (and still are) noted for the quality of their pottery, "thin and smooth, glazed, and with colours shading into one another." There was some gold in the Omagua villages as well, but the Spanish, more interested in getting out of the area alive than in getting rich, left it alone.

Curiously though, the chroniclers of this trip failed to mention two other particular characteristics of the Omagua. One was that they flattened their children's heads so that they bulged sideways, not unlike the heads of hammerhead sharks. The other was that the Omagua were the first people in the world to use wild rubber and made both boots and syringes from it!

It was in mid-February 1542 that the expedition reached the main branch of the river now known as the Amazon. John Hemming described the river as seen by Orellana and his men as they slowly traveled down the river, quoted by Norma Gaffron:

> *The Amazon near the Omagua lands is as broad as a lake, and its mass of gently flowing water is the colour of an Indian's skin. The banks are unbroken walls of dark green vegetation, with the great trees masked by a screen of undergrowth. These endless lines of tree-tops are now interrupted only by the occasional mud bank; but in Orellana's day there were frequent Indian villages, with long lines of huts along the water's edge . . . There are occasional floating logs of*

islands of grass, a fish breaking the surface, tributaries making brief openings in the curtain wall of trees, or flights of macaws, herons, toucans or eagles watching the edges of the river. Otherwise, for day after day, there was only the immensely broad, placid river and the unbroken lines of trees.

The 2,000-kilometer (1,242-mile) journey was, not surprisingly, filled with adventures around every corner, as new territories were entered and new tribes were encountered. Sometimes they were attacked. Sometimes they attacked small villages in order to steal food.

On one particularly memorable occasion, after being menaced by a number of native canoes, the Spanish decided to land onshore and attack

A PETITION TO FRANCISCO DE ORELLANA

When reading history books, it often seems that a leader and his men are always working together for the same goal: The leader leads, his men follow, and they all have the same drive and determination to make history. But that is not always the case. When Francisco de Orellana first ordered his men to make preparations to go back upriver to bring desperately needed supplies to Gonzalo Pizarro, he received the following petition, dated January 4, 1542, quoted by Robert Silverberg and signed by 49 of his men, with the name of Friar Gaspar de Carvajal at the head of the list:

We, the cavaliers and hidalgos and priests who are here with this expeditionary force with Your Worship, having become aware of Your Worship's determination to go up the river over the course down which we came with Your Worship, and having seen that is an impossible thing to go back up to where Your Worship left Gonzalo Pizarro, our Governor, without risking the lives of us all . . . Therefore we beseech Your Worship, and we beg him and summon him, not to take us with him back up the river.

The petitioners humbly added,

the village. The Spanish were astonished by the ferocious defense put up by the villagers, who fought on tirelessly with nothing more than bows and arrows, even as their numbers were rapidly diminishing under the onslaught of Spanish guns and crossbows.

One Spanish victim, Dominican friar Gaspar de Carvajal, was hit by an arrow that pierced his rib cage. In his chronicle of the event, he became convinced that the reason the villagers were so determined to defend their land was because they were ruled by a tribe of warrior women, known through myth and legend as Amazons. Carvajal wrote:

We ourselves saw ten or twelve of these women, fighting there in front of all the Indian men as female captains. They fought so

> *We hereby exonerate ourselves from the charge of being traitors or even men disobedient to the service of the King in not follow-ing Your Worship on this journey.*

Orellana, faced with such opposition from his men, had little choice. The very next day, he issued a response to the petitioners, granting their request, saying, according to Silverberg, that,

> *. . . inasmuch as it was impossible to go back up the river again, he was ready, although against his desire, to look for another route to bring them out as a port of rescue.*

Does this mean that Pizarro's accusations of being abandoned by Orellana were unfounded? Not necessarily. Although the petition and the follow-up response were carefully preserved by Orellana to protect his reputation, there are those who believe that he did not have to be pushed hard to abandon Pizarro and go on to explore the length of the Amazon. And there are those who believe that both the petition and follow-up were written up *after* the fact to prove that he had no choice in the matter!

courageously that the men did not dare turn their backs. They killed any [Indian men] who did turn back, with their clubs, right there in front of us, which is why the Indians kept up their defences for so long. These women are very white and tall, with very long braided hair wound about their heads. They are very robust, and go naked with their private parts covered, with bows and arrows in their hands, doing as much fighting as ten Indian men ... And indeed there was one woman among these who shot an arrow a span (about nine inches) into one of the brigantines [boats]; others did the same until our brigantines looked like porcupines.

Indeed, according to Carvajal, one captured Indian told him that he had visited the villages of the warrior women, about a week's march north of the river. His account reminded Orellana of the Greek legend of the Amazons, a race of warlike women who did not allow men to live with them. Carvajal began referring to these women as "Amazons" and, eventually, renamed the river after them.

Carvajal, according to his own account, was fascinated by what the captured Indian had to tell him about the tribe of women warriors:

The Indian said that their [the women warriors] houses were of stone and with regular doors, and that from one village to another went roads ... with guards stationed at intervals along them so that no one might enter without paying duty. The Captain asked if these women bore children: the Indian answered that they did. He asked them how, not being married, and there being no man residing among them, they became pregnant; he replied that these Indian women consorted with Indian men at times, when desire came over them. They also assembled a great horde of warriors and went off to make war on a very great chieftain whose residence is not far from the land of these women, and so by force they brought them to their own country and kept them with them for the time that suited their caprice, and after they found themselves pregnant they sent them back to their country without doing them any harm. Afterwards, when the time came for them to have children, if they gave birth to male children they killed them or sent them to their fathers, and if females, they raised them in the arts of war.

Carvajal said he had an eyewitness who swore that the Amazons were real. Noted historian John Hemming didn't think so and noted that the witness all-too-readily agreed with every preconceived idea put to him by his captors—the picture of the Amazons that he drew seemed to be too exact a replica of the Amazons of ancient legend.

No other chronicler of the time believed the account either, with Lopez de Gomara angrily stating, "No such thing has ever been seen along this river, and never will be seen! Because of this imposture many already write and talk of the 'River of the Amazons.'" Even so, to this day, the world's largest river continues to be named after this mythical tribe of sexually liberated warrior women.

The Spanish endured more battles along the way. In an attempt to raid a village for food, Friar Carvajal's eye was pierced by an arrow. By late July they were close to the mouth of the river, where they spent some time refitting their boats and gathering supplies for their voyage up the Atlantic coast.

The two brigs reached the island of Margarita, off the coast of Venezuela, on September 9 and 11, 1542. They had accomplished what no European had done; it was one of the world's great explorations, described by Fernandez de Oviedo as "something more than a shipwreck, more than a miraculous event."

Orellana returned to Spain to report on his discoveries and to raise the necessary money to launch yet another expedition. Given the stories he had to tell, the funds were made available to him, and so, now with the official title of governor of the Amazons, he set out again with a crew of 500 men to search for El Dorado.

But once again, El Dorado remained undiscovered. Francisco de Orellana died onboard ship on his return journey, within sight of the Amazon River, which he named. And so, Orellana's name was added to the growing list of explorers who died in search of a legend.

Antonio de Berrio

Despite the failure of Pizarro's expedition, and Orellana's expedition, and those of so many others, there were still those determined to do what they couldn't do, and find the legendary area known as El Dorado.

Expedition after expedition, explorer after explorer, would-be conquistador after would-be conquistador set out into the jungles of the upper Amazon valley, only to come to grief as the tropical heat, exhaustion, disease, starvation, and hostile Indians destroyed one dream of gold after another. No one, it seemed, had come any closer to discovering El Dorado.

John Hemming wrote "the supposed location of El Dorado and his kingdom withdrew farther and farther into the remaining, unexplored portion of the interior. Finally, there was nowhere left for it to be found except in the dim fastnesses of 'Guiana,' the name by which the Spaniards knew the great unmapped basin of the Orinoco [River] and its tributaries." The words "El Dorado" had become a siren's call, luring hapless explorers to fail in the jungles of the Amazon. For one such conquistador, it became his life's mission.

THE THREE JOURNEYS OF De BERRIO

Antonio de Berrio was born in 1520, the same year that Cortés began his march on Mexico. A military man, he fought at Siena, against the Barbary pirates; in Germany; in the Netherlands; and in Granada. Two of his brothers had died in battle with him, and a third brother died at Lepanto, a famous Catholic naval victory against the Turks.

Consumed with his career, Berrio did not marry until the age of 53 or 54, but the wait proved to be advantageous to him. His wife was the niece of none other than our old acquaintance Gonzalo Jimenez de Quesada. Quesada, despite the failure of his expedition in search of El Dorado, had made his fortune founding the Spanish kingdom of New Grenada in what is roughly today's Colombia.

When Quesada died in 1579, his estates in New Grenada were inherited by his niece, and through her, to Antonio de Berrio. Now retired at the age of 60, with a five-year-old daughter and a two-year-old son, Berrio and family set sail in 1580 to claim their inheritance. It seems likely that Berrio saw this as an opportunity to completely retire away from the claims of the Spanish military and enjoy the rich estates he was now in control of, not to mention the yearly income of 14,000 ducats he'd be receiving.

But when he arrived, he discovered that a life of sea breezes and relaxation were not going to be possible. There was a clause in Quesada's will that required Berrio to "most insistently" continue the search for El Dorado. Berrio, always a man of duty, realized he had no time to rest and jumped back into the saddle. As he wrote years later, the search had become his life,

> *The circumstances and my own inclination were sufficient of themselves to persuade me to it; and so I decided to make ready and set forth quest thereof. I collected a large force of men and a great quantity of horses, cattle, munitions, and other necessary stores; and with this equipment, which cost me a great deal of gold, I started.*

As V.S. Naipaul noted in his book *The Loss of El Dorado*, those preparations, which Berrio set down in just one sentence, had taken three years.

The question though is this: Berrio was old and rich, he didn't need the money, and could easily have hired others to do the search for him. Why did he go himself? Alvin Schwartz, in his book *Gold & Silver, Silver & Gold*, quoted by Gaffron, may have an answer when he said, "Everyone who hunts for treasure dreams of striking it rich. But often it is more than money that attracts them. It is the hunt itself."

There were three journeys in all. The first one lasted 17 months, and men died. The second one came to an end after 28 months. Berrio wrote "While I was having canoes made to travel down this river, a captain mutinied and fled with the majority of his men, so that I was obliged to start after him."

Naipaul observed that in Berrio's narrative, time vanishes, "like effort, like the landscape itself." Finally Berrio is ready to begin his third journey. Ten years have passed since his arrival in New Granada. He is now 70 years old. He has six daughters. His son is now twelve years old and joins his father on what has become known as Berrio's great journey. It was the journey that Berrio looked back on time and time again, not, as Naipaul pointed out, because of what he had seen or because of the continent that he had crossed, but "because half-way across he had performed a deed which linked him in his own mind with the heroes of antiquity."

The dream was to go down the Orinoco River to what were thought to be the highlands of El Dorado. From the river they would go on land to search out the mountain pass that Berrio was certain was all that separated him from the golden city. It was a small expedition, fewer than 120 men, along with a limited number of slaves. Half the men traveled on the river in canoes with Berrio; the other half remained on land, moving along the riverbank with 200 horses, under the command of a soldier who had served with Quesada.

They traveled this way for a year. No entryway into the mountains was found. When the rainy season came, they camped on the flooded banks of the Orinoco. That's when the trouble started. Berrio wrote that,

> *The canoes had been lost, and three troops of Spaniards, thirty-four men in all, deserted, taking many horses with them. A disease almost like the plague killed all my porters and more than thirty Spaniards.*

It was then that Berrio sprang into action, performing the action that, in his mind at least, linked him to the heroes of old. To prevent further soldiers from deserting and making it impossible for them to return to New Granada, Berrio ordered the remaining horses to be killed. After eating the horse meat, additional canoes were hollowed out from tree trunks, and the journey down the river continued.

They came to Carib country. Caribs were actual cannibals who, twice a year, sent fleets of up to 30 canoes up and down the river hunting for fresh human meat; for a distance of 350 leagues (slightly over 1,000 miles [1,609 km]) the Caribs' hunting ground had been depopulated,

Bound by honor and obligation, Antonio de Berrio continued the search for El Dorado on behalf of his wife's uncle, the great explorer Jimenez de Quesada. On his way down the Orinoco River, Berrio and his men encountered the Carib, a tribe known for hunting and eating humans. *Above*, a tribe from the upper Orinoco River region grills the legs of a human.

fully eaten out. Fortunately for Berrio, the Caribs he met were friendly, offered him and his men food, and, at least according to Berrio's later account, also offered to guide him part of the way to El Dorado, which they did, to the mouth of the Caroni River, into the territory of a chief called Moriquito.

Moriquito was already aware of the Spanish presence in South America, so Berrio knew that he was getting close to the coast and Spanish settlements. Moriquito informed him that it was only an additional four-day march to El Dorado, but Berrio turned down the offer, not wanting to find the treasure along with Moriquito, and, besides,

> *I had only fifty soldiers, and only fifteen of these were in good health. I couldn't leave the canoes either, because if these were lost all was lost.*

LOPE DE AGUIRRE

There were many men—explorers, would-be conquistadors, vision-aries—who went into the wilds of South America in search of gold and fame, but few established a reputation for cruelty and madness that rivaled that of Lupe de Aguirre.

Aguirre (c. 1510–October 27, 1561) was in his twenties and living in Seville, Spain, when Hernando Pizarro returned from Peru, bringing with him the treasures of the Incan Empire and inspiring Aguirre to go to South America to discover his own El Dorado.

He arrived in Peru in 1537 and quickly made a name for himself as a trainer of horses, as well as for his violence and cruelty as a conquistador. He also became known for his sheer stubbornness, spending three years and traveling 6,000 kilometers (3,728 miles) on foot to hunt down a judge whom he felt had wronged him. (When he finally caught up with the judge, he killed him by cutting his temples and then watched him bleed to death.)

Few stories of stubbornness though, match his fruitless search for El Dorado.

Along with his daughter Alvira, he joined the 1560 expedition of Pedro de Ursua down the Maranon and Amazon rivers along with

After five more of his men became ill, and a quarrel with Moriquito about food threatened the safety of his men, Berrio decided to move on.

His goal now was merely to survive, to get out of the Orinoco and find the nearest Spanish settlement.

> I went down the Orinoco to the sea. This river goes out by so many arms and narrow channels that it inundates a two-hundred league stretch of coast for more than forty leagues inland. The arm by which I came out faces the island of Trinidad, which is four leagues from the mainland. I was determined to remain there and to settle the island, and to reassemble my men in order to enter Guiana again. But God and my fortune willed it that as soon as we were in the sea we were separated. The vessels were small and the soldiers ill and

300 men and hundreds of natives. Just a year later he took over the expedition, participating in the overthrow and killing of Ursua and his successor, Fernando de Guzman.

Aguirre and his men reached the Atlantic, albeit without finding El Dorado, destroying native villages all along the way. In March 23, 1561, Aguirre urged 186 captains and soldiers to sign a document proclaiming him as prince of Peru, Tierra Firma, and Chile.

He is reported to have said in 1561:

I am the Wrath of God the Prince of Freedom Lord of Tierra Firme and the Provinces of Chile

Later in 1561, he took control of Isla Margarita, brutally killing anyone who dared to oppose his reign. But when he crossed over to the mainland in an attempt to conquer Panama, his days came to an end. He was surrounded by Spanish troops at Barquisimeto, Venezuela, where he murdered his own daughter before he himself was captured and killed. His body was cut into quarters and sent to four different cities across Venezuela.

inexperienced and unable to row. I arrived in Trinidad with twenty men and stayed there for eight days, although all my men were ill.

After choosing sites for new settlements, Berrio and his men made the last stretch of journey to the island of Margarita.

They had been traveling for a year and a half, and he arrived in Margarita a broken and exhausted man. Waiting for him was the news that his wife had died in New Granada while he was away, leaving two sons and seven daughters. Still, despite everything, Berrio was unwilling or unable to give up on his dreams of El Dorado. He sent his oldest son, now 14 years old, to Caracas and then on to New Granada to get more men and supplies for yet another expedition. His son, however, gave up on the quest and remained safely home in New Granada.

ANOTHER TALE EMERGES

Berrio, suffering from intermittent fevers, remained on Margarita as the guest of the island's governor. He even wrote to the king of Spain, praising the young governor's generosity and kindness, not knowing that at the same time, the governor was also writing to the king, offering to lead an expedition to find El Dorado himself and calling Berrio an old fool.

Berrio, not knowing the governor's intentions, wanted to return to the search himself. He promised the governor half of his marquisate in return for his help, but the governor refused. Berrio, in reality, had nothing to offer him.

Why, though, would Berrio—sick, tired, and now over 70 years old—be willing to lead one more expedition into the wild in search of El Dorado? A new story had emerged from the jungles of South America, of a man named Albujar who after 16 years had suddenly emerged from the jungle, the sole surviving member of a lost and forgotten El Dorado expedition. This man, Albujar, according to the stories that quickly spread through the area, claimed to have actually seen the golden city with his own eyes.

It was said that Albujar had been in charge of his expedition's munitions. The munitions had blown up, and for his punishment, Albujar had been sentenced to death by being set adrift alone down the Orinoco River. The rest of his expedition was attacked and killed by Indians, but, according to the stories, Albujar was rescued and saved.

He was, he claimed, brought by his rescuers blindfolded on a two-week-long journey, at the end of which the blindfold was removed and he found himself in the Great Manoa, the city of the golden man. The city itself was so large it took an entire day to walk from the city gates to the main gate to the palace of the ruler. There, he claimed, he saw "with his own eyes" the Gilded Man and his court as the legends had said, with their skin glistening with gold.

Albujar claimed he remained there for seven months, answering the Gilded Man's questions about the white men, before being released. Then, his eyes covered with a blindfold, he was escorted back through the jungle, loaded with gifts of gold and jewels. While making his way back through the jungle, Albujar claimed that the gold and jewels were stolen, leaving him with nothing but a few gold beads. All he could do to prove his story was to show those to people and offer to swear on the Bible that he was telling the truth.

Was the story true? Had Albujar found the golden city that so many had sought for in vain, or had his time alone in the jungles of South America simply driven him mad? Did he even exist at all? Writer V.S. Naipaul, for one, is not sure.

> *Albujar may never have existed. No one saw him, and the story was that he didn't live long after his return. He died in Puerto Rico, waiting for a ship to Spain. No one saw the gold beads; they were left with Albujar's confessor to pay for masses.*

But as Naipaul went on to say, the search for El Dorado and its gold was becoming more than just a search. It was becoming "a New World romance, a dream of Shangri-La, the complete unviolated world." The

The Spaniards, having pillaged and settled South America, longed for more undiscovered lands and tales of treasure and hoped that someone would find El Dorado. Despite three previously unsuccessful expeditions, Berrio was convinced he could find the mysterious city and sent a crew to claim the land around the Orinoco River.

Sir Walter Raleigh and the End of the Quest

Little is known about the early life of Walter Raleigh. Although some historians believe he was born in 1552, it seems more likely that he was born in 1554, the son of a farmer, near Devon, England.

He was a man determined to make something of himself and to make himself known. It is known that he spent time in Ireland, taking part in the suppression of Irish rebellions against British rule, participating in the infamous massacres at Rathlin Island and Smerwick. He became a major landowner for his efforts, receiving 40,000 acres of land in Munster. He made plans to build settlements in the "Colony and Dominion of Virginia," plans that included failed settlements at Roanoke Island in 1584 and 1587.

Even with the failure of the Roanoke colonies, Raleigh rose quickly in the favor of Queen Elizabeth as one of her favored courtiers and poets, earning his knighthood in 1585. But in 1591, after he secretly married Elizabeth Throckmorton, one of the queen's ladies-in-waiting, the queen, who may or may not have been in love with him, ordered him imprisoned in the infamous Tower of London. As author Marc Aronson noted in his biography, *Sir Walter Raleigh and the Quest for El Dorado*, "Elizabeth reacted as both a jealous lover and a vengeful ruler out to crush disloyalty."

He was saved from the Tower when his men captured the Portuguese ship *Madre de Dios*, which contained more than 537 tons of spices, in addition to pearls, silks, ivory, silver, and gold, with an estimated value of over half a million pounds. Raleigh was the only man who could keep the captured goods safe and divide them appropriately. With a payment of 80,000 pounds to the queen, his freedom was ensured.

Raleigh may have been free, but he no longer had the queen's trust, confidence, or love. The one way he could win it back, he was certain, was to win enough land and treasure in her name that she would once again grant him her favor. He would have to find El Dorado.

Timothy Severin wrote that Raleigh "went about the matter thoroughly." He searched out any piece of information he could find about El Dorado and the Gilded Man, questioning both captains and the passengers of every ship arriving from Spain's colonies in the Americas. He searched libraries as well, reading all of the Spanish chronicles written up to that time, chronicles which, as we have seen, were filled with the stories and legends of a golden kingdom in the jungle.

The last pieces fell into place for Raleigh in 1594, when an English ship under the command of Captain George Popham intercepted a Spanish ship. Among the documents seized by the British were letters that spelled out all available evidence supporting the theory of El Dorado, including the recent "discoveries" of Domingo de Vera.

Raleigh, though, was driven by more than "just" gold. That same year, Raleigh received news that Antonio de Berrio had ambushed and killed eight English sailors who had gone ashore in Trinidad hunting for fresh meat. Not only did this seem to prove to Raleigh that Berrio was close to conquering El Dorado, but also that it was in the interest of the English crown to make sure that the Spanish did not have access to the treasures on their own.

Indeed, as Severin pointed out, "The truth of the matter was, that Raleigh . . . was aiming at no less than a complete English empire in South America, and already he had a name for it—'Guiana,' the word which Juan Martinez de Albujar had used in connection with the Gilded Man."

Queen Elizabeth I, no longer in love with Raleigh, did not care whether or not he remained in England and granted him an official commission, ordering him to "offend and enfeeble the King of Spain." The only thing blocking Raleigh from his dream was 74-year-old Antonio de Berrio.

RALEIGH GOES ON THE HUNT

He didn't block him for long. Raleigh was thrilled when he and his men arrived in Trinidad, reveling in the "curiosities" to be seen. When he and

Sir Walter Raleigh, a favorite of Queen Elizabeth, was investing in the Virginia colony in the New World when he heard about El Dorado. Raleigh was one of the few non-Spanish explorers to venture into South America and later published a book detailing his experiences.

his men saw Berrio and his men, he sent a boatload of food and drink to the Spaniards who were guarding the island's landing place. While these men were enjoying their repast, Raleigh's men surrounded and killed them all.

Berrio was taken prisoner, and his captor told him of his determination to find El Dorado, leaving Berrio, according to Raleigh as cited by Aronson, "stricken into a great melancholy and sadness." Berrio tried to tell Raleigh that the trip was not worth taking, that he and his crew would suffer "many miseries" in the jungle, that the rivers were too shallow to sail, and that the natives would not be forthcoming with information or food or gold. Raleigh of course, assumed that Berrio was telling him all this to stop him from finding the Golden City himself. But in a later account of the trip, he admitted that most of Berrio's warnings were true.

The two men, the 71-year-old Spanish conquistador and the 41-year-old English would-be discoverer of El Dorado, were two of a kind, both chasing the same dream. Each of them was convinced that the other's interest meant that El Dorado was close at hand, that the myths and legends they both knew so well were within their reach. The only way to find out for sure, though, would be to enter the jungle.

Sir Walter Raleigh was gone from Trinidad for 30 days, half of that time spent getting from the Gulf of Paria to the main Orinoco. The first Indian he picked up to be his guide was polite, but as it turned out, had forgotten his way. Raleigh wrote:

> And if God had not send us another helpe, we might have wandered a whole yere in that labyrinth of rivers, yer wee had found any way, either out or in.

Another Indian, who had been captured by chance, turned out to be capable of leading Raleigh and his men into the Orinoco.

Raleigh was fortunate in that news of the killings of the Spaniards met with approval by the Indians on the Orinoco, and in Moriquito's territory he was regarded as a liberator from the much-hated Spanish. And in order to keep the peace, Raleigh made sure his men knew not to steal anything from the locals, not to abuse their power or make advances toward any women. Perhaps in gratitude, an elderly cacique named Topiawari told Raleigh what he wanted to hear, telling him the story he had heard in his youth, of Incas who "came from so far off as the sun slept," and of the mountains of Guiana and the city of gold. Raleigh recounted the story:

> *. . . there came down into that large valley of Guiana, a nation from so far off as the Sun slept (for such were his own words) with so great a multitude as they could not be numbered or resisted, & and that they wore large coats, and hats of crimson color . . . those that had slain and rooted out so many of the ancient people as there were leaves in the wood upon all the trees, and had now made themselves Lord of all . . . built a great town . . . and that their houses have many rooms, one over the other, and therein the great king . . . kept three thousand men to defend the borders against them . . .*

Of course, as was usually the case, the cacique did not know the exact route that would lead through the mountains to the golden kingdom. The best he could (or would) do was to advise Raleigh and his men to continue traveling upstream until they reached the mouth of the Caroni, a large tributary that branched off to the right of the Orinoco. The Caroni, Topiawari assured Raleigh, was the beginning of the way to El Dorado.

This was, as we have seen time and time again, the kind of vague promise that would-be explorer after would-be explorer had heard from Indian after Indian. Were they telling the invaders of their land what they knew? Were they telling them what they thought they wanted to hear? Were they telling them anything they could to encourage them to keep moving out of their lands, to an El Dorado that was always over the next mountain? Or, is it possible that Raleigh made up the entire story himself? That is something we will never know for sure.

What we do know is that when Raleigh reached the confluence of the Orinoco and the Caroni, that was as far as he went before going back downstream to return to his ships and men in Trinidad. Why didn't he continue to go forward?

Upon his return to England, Raleigh told the men who had backed his journey that the rising flood waters in the Orinoco made it impossible for him to go any farther. He also insisted that he needed to get back to his men waiting for him at Point Icacos, at the mouth of the Orinoco. He had spent no more than six days among the Indians of the Orinoco.

He arrived back in England seven months after he left, returning with nothing more than some Indian artifacts, some tobacco, some rocks that may or may not have contained gold ore, and a new collection of stories about the golden land of El Dorado, stories that he soon published that would spread the story of El Dorado even farther.

GUIANA

Not surprisingly, Raleigh did not receive a hero's welcome upon his return home to Britain. His financial backers were unhappy with how little he had brought back, and his political enemies, some of whom claimed he had never left England at all, rejoiced in his failure. To make matters worse, the "gold ore" he had brought back from the Caroni turned out not to be gold at all.

In order to preserve his reputation, Raleigh wrote an account of his journey, known as *The Discovery of Guiana*. Raleigh had been a talented poet, and the book was beautifully written, but its accuracy has long been debated. Take, for example, his story about the Ewaipanoma Indian tribe.

Raleigh described them as a freakish tribe of club-wielding giants living in isolation in Guiana. He, of course, had never seen any of them, but he heard stories from the Orinoco Indians that they actually existed. According to the Orinoco, these giants were monsters with no heads, whose eyes, noses, and mouths were located in the middle of their chests! To top it off, their long hair grew backward from their shoulders.

Not only was the story not true, but the story of "headless giants" had been floating around Europe for more than a thousand years, even appearing in one of the earliest "travel" books ever written, Sir John Mandeville's *Travels*. Why did Raleigh choose to resurrect such a dusty tale, replant it in South America, and call it his own? Raleigh knew that his tall tales would attract attention to his book.

Indeed, the book was a huge, popular success, although it seemed to fail with the people whose support Raleigh needed the most: financial backers and Queen Elizabeth. The book was published throughout Europe, extending the reach of Raleigh's curious mix of fact, half-truths, and fantasies about the New World. One useful item that Raleigh *was* able to provide was a remarkably accurate map, depicting the large section of South America that lay between the mouth of the Amazon and the Isthmus of Panama.

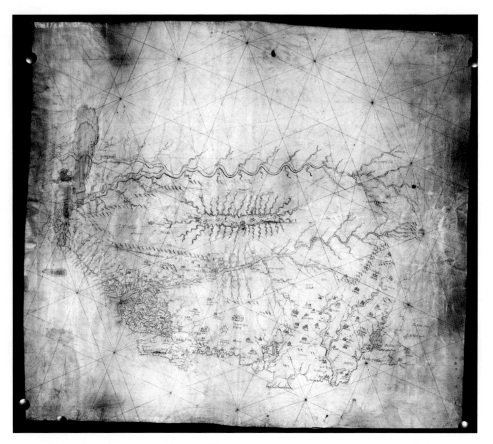

Raleigh's book, *The Discovery of Guiana*, was wildly popular with the public, but much of the information was fabricated or completely made up. Although there was a detailed map of South America included in the book, Raleigh had drawn in a fictional lake and claimed that cities of gold were located on its shores.

But even that map, which was as precise as any map of the time, was marred by Raleigh's fantasies. There, located just behind the line of the "mountains of Guinana" was drawn the outline of a large lake, placed between the Amazon and Orinoco rivers. It was called the Lake of Manoa, and according to Raleigh, on its shores were all of the golden cities of legend, including the one known to the Spanish as El Dorado. This lake, which did not exist, also known as Lake Parima, remained on maps until the 1800s.

Raleigh's hope to make a quick return to Guiana and El Dorado was dashed when, in 1603, he was arrested, accused of plotting against Britain's new king, James I, and convicted of treason. Only his eloquence saved him from immediate execution, and he was sent back to the Tower of London.

During his time in the Tower, Raleigh sent a ship to the Orinoco delta every year in order to stay in contact with the Orinoco Indians and keep informed about the Spaniards' progress in their search for El Dorado. He learned from his aide, Captain Keymis, that the Spanish had fortified their positions all along the Caroni River because, Keymis insisted, they had opened gold mines there. The Spanish, on the other hand, were hoping to find the gold that they believed had brought Raleigh into the area. The actions of each side only seemed to confirm to the other side that there was gold there to be found.

Raleigh remained in the Tower until 1616, when James I, desperately in need of funds, finally agreed to release him in order to return to Venezuela in search of El Dorado. There were two conditions: Raleigh must return to England with gold. And, on the pain of death, he or his men were not to physically harm any Spaniards they should encounter in any way. It was Raleigh's final opportunity to redeem himself, to prove to the world that his book was true, that El Dorado was there, just where he claimed it would be.

But his second expedition was an unmitigated disaster. Raleigh's plan was to sneak past the Spanish fortifications along the Orinoco. Along with Raleigh were his son Walter (known as Wat) and his longtime aide and friend, Keymis. But when Raleigh became seriously ill with a fever en route and was unable to lead the actual on-land expedition in search of the mine, Wat and Keymis were left to lead the British upstream.

Wat, known for being as reckless as his father, attacked a Spanish fort and was killed. When Keymis returned to the ship with the news that there was no mine and no gold, and his beloved son Wat was dead along with several Spaniards, Raleigh knew that the worst had happened: he was doomed. Keymis killed himself in despair. Raleigh, instead of fleeing or remaining in the New World, returned home to meet his fate, knowing, at last, that El Dorado was not there for him to find. He was beheaded on October 29, 1618.

It was, in many ways, the end of the search. Raleigh's last voyage proved once and for all the myth of El Dorado and exposed it, as Aronson wrote, for what it was: "a European dream that had become a nightmare, a madness, a questing after phantoms that only grew ever more destructive the more hopeless it had become."

SIR WALTER RALEIGH: WRITER

Although best known as a soldier, explorer, and courtier to Queen Elizabeth I, Sir Walter Raleigh was also known as a fine writer for his history books, *The Discovery of Guiana* and his *History of the World*, which explored the history of ancient Greece and Rome.

Today, though, his reputation as a writer rests largely on his poetry, a body of work noted for its relatively straightforward and unornamented style. Of particular note is this poem, written the night before his beheading on Friday, October 29, 1618.

SIR WALTER RALEIGH (The Night Before His Death)

Even such is time, which takes in trust
  Our youth, our joys, and all we have,
  And pays us nought but age and dust;
  Which in the dark and silent grave,
  When we have wandered all our ways,
  Shuts up the story of our days!
  And from which grave, and earth, and dust,
  The Lord shall raise me up, I trust.

With Raleigh's death, it was clear that there *were* no golden kingdoms to be found on the continent of South America. All there was were legends and myths and stories and dreams all wrapped up together in the minds of would-be conquistadors. Raleigh, by giving up everything in search of a dream, proved the destructiveness of the dream and, in the process, made himself a true tragic hero.

AFTER THE DREAM DIED

The dream of El Dorado had lured explorers deep into South America, from the Andes into what are now Peru, Ecuador, and Colombia, into Venezuela and Brazil, meaning, as Caspar Montibell wrote in *The Search for Eldorado*, as quoted by Gaffron, "The road to El Dorado was littered with corpses of captains, soldiers, and Indians. Except for a few nuggets of gold, a sizeable haul of emeralds and some cinnamon, there was little to show for nearly a century of exploration. No one had found the Golden Man or discovered his treasure."

But although the "Golden Man" was never found, there was a lot more gold found than just "a few nuggets." Literally tons of gold made its way back to Europe from Central and South America—enough gold to ensure that even though the dream of a Golden Man and a golden city faded, the search for gold and treasure never ended.

And, interestingly, evidence was found that seemed to indicate that some of the stories of El Dorado were based, albeit loosely, on reality. In 1580, Antonio Sepulveda received permission from the Spanish crown to drain Lake Guatavita, to determine if it was true that the Muisca had made offerings in the sacred lake. Eight thousand Indian workers were assembled to dig a giant notch in the rim of the lake.

After months of digging it worked, and a torrent of water gushed out of the V-shaped notch, unfortunately taking a good number of Indian laborers with it. Along the edge of the lake, 232 pesos and 10 grams of gold were all that were found. It was enough to prove perhaps that some sort of ceremonies had taken place in the lake, but not enough to prove the tales of great sacrifices of gold and jewels.

But few were immune to the dream of gold. Even noted naturalist Alexander von Humboldt, while exploring the area around Bogota in 1809, visited Lake Guatavita and commented on Sepulveda's cut, which was (and still is) a prominent part of the landscape. He noted that the banks of the lake seemed to show the remains of a staircase, which, he claimed, were used in religious ceremonies.

When he returned to Paris, Humboldt calculated that if a thousand Indians had made a yearly pilgrimage to Guatavita over the course of 100 years, and, as the stories claimed, had thrown a minimum of five golden pieces into the lake to honor the local deity, there should be upward of 50,000,000 golden pieces buried in the thick black ooze that lined the bottom of the lake. The thought of that much gold inspired "Pepe" Paris of Bogota to make another attempt to empty the lake, but again, nothing more could be found.

Was it possible then, that Guatavita was not the only sacred lake used by the Muisca? There were, it turned out, other lakes that the Muisca considered sacred, centers for pilgrimage where shrines were built and offerings made. Was it possible that treasure could be found there?

Lake Siecha, a round lake just south of the village of Guatavita, was seen as a likely candidate. In 1856, a channel was dug into the lake that lowered it by more than 11 feet (3.3 m). Some Muisca items were found, including one that led many to believe that the stories of El Dorado were true. What was discovered along the edge of the lake was a replica all in gold of a raft with a tall central figure and ten attendants. Could this golden raft indicate that the stories of religious ceremonies involving sacrifices of gold and jewels into the lake were true? John Hemming, former director of the Royal Geographical Society and author of *The Search for El Dorado*, thinks not:

> *It is important to place this raft in perspective. It evidently portrays a ceremony on a lake. But it is only one of thousands of surviving gold Muisca artifacts. Worship of lakes was only one element in Muisca religion. The first observers of Muisca society wrote much about its religion but scarcely mentioned the importance of lakes, for the Muisca worshipped mountains, celestial bodies, ancestors, and the magnificent rock gorges and outcrops that make the scenery around Bogota so exciting. The Muisca did not produce gold: they traded it from other tribes, and their gold objects tended to be small as a result. They could not have afforded the prodigal waste of gold dust described in El Dorado legends. Thus, although there was religious significance in the mysterious Lake Guatavita, it was not central to Muisca beliefs. It is difficult to see how it could have given rise to the powerful El Dorado legend . . .*

Spurred on by the discovery of the 7.5-inch-long (19 centimeter) golden raft, attempts were made throughout the nineteenth century and even into the twentieth to force Lake Guatavita and other surrounding lakes to reveal their secrets, but to no avail. If El Dorado had been in the area as so many stories promised and as so many explorers believed, it was not to be found.

Obviously, other golden cities had been found, and in the quest much gold had been shipped back to Europe and many men had become rich. Even so, for whatever reason, El Dorado, no matter how close Berrio, Raleigh, and countless others had come to it, had remained forever out of reach. Is it because it never existed? Or . . . were all those would-be conquistadors and explorers simply looking in the wrong place?

THE LOST CITY OF Z

While most maps showed "El Dorado" located somewhere between Venezuela and Colombia, other maps indicated the possible location for El Dorado extended farther south, deeper in the wilds of Brazil. This area, known as the Matto Grosso, is considered to be the heart of the South American continent. And to some, in this largely unexplored area, lay the remains of the legendary city of El Dorado.

Famed British explorer Percy Fawcett was convinced that a lost city he called Z, a modern version of El Dorado, once existed in an unexplored area of South America. He and his traveling companions disappeared without a trace in 1925, further extending the myth of the ancient golden city.

One man who believed that was famed British explorer Colonel Percy Harrison Fawcett. A onetime spy and veteran of World War I, he became convinced, based on years of research, fieldwork, and wishful thinking, that deep in the jungles of the Amazon were the ruins of a lost civilization.

But for centuries this possibility had seemed an impossibility. The area was considered to be a primeval wilderness, a merciless jungle that was simply too inhospitable to support a large civilized population. In the early 1900s, Percy Fawcett decided to challenge that notion.

While exploring and mapping an area in Bolivia along with polar explorer James Murray, Fawcett reported finding large mounds of earth, each filled with pottery. He also claimed that he had found, buried under the floor of the jungle, traces of causeways and roadways. As implausible as it seemed, Fawcett insisted that his find proved that the Amazon once contained and supported large populations and at least one, perhaps even more, advanced civilizations.

His findings shocked the world and inspired Sir Arthur Conan Doyle (the creator of Sherlock Homes) to write his classic *The Lost World* in 1912. Fawcett was certain he was on the trail of something big, and after carefully reading all of the early Spanish chronicles of exploration, he knew what it was he was looking for. As quoted in David Grann's modern bestseller, *The Lost City of Z*:

> *The central place I call "Z"—our main objective—is in a valley . . . about ten miles wide, and the city is on an eminence in the middle of it, approached by a barreled roadway of stone. The houses are low and windowless, and there is a pyramidial temple.*

When Fawcett, along with his son Jack and Jack's best friend, Raleigh Rimell, set out to find the lost city in 1925, they captured the imagination of the world. One newspaper, quoted by Grann, wrote, "Not since the days of Ponce de León crossed unknown Florida in search of the Waters of Perpetual Youth . . . has a more alluring adventure been planned." For one month, Indian runners were used to carry back reports of his progress into Amazonia, stories that were published in newspapers all around the world. Then, suddenly, the messages stopped.

Fawcett was never heard from again. Had he been killed by locals? Had he been eaten by animals or even cannibals? Or, had he found his paradise in the jungle, the lost city of Z of myth and legend, and decided never to return back to "civilization"? Numerous parties went in search for the answers to those questions, and more than 100 people are said to have died in the process. But the fate of Fawcett and his city of "Z" remained lost in the jungle.

And while Fawcett's fate has not been discovered, in a story that made headlines in early 2010, a report in the journal *Antiquity* by the archeologist Martii Parssinen and others proved that Fawcett was right. Using satellite imagery researchers have found, in areas of the upper Amazon basin cleared by deforestation in the very area where Fawcett searched and then vanished, the remains of a vast and complex civilization, complete with geometrically aligned roads and structures.

To date, more than 200 earthworks, some built as late as the thirteenth century, others dating back two centuries before Christ, have been found. The remains of houses, moats, roads, bridges, avenues, and squares, all lined out with startling geometric precision, have been located—twenty settlements in all, each with populations estimated to be anywhere between 2,000 to 5,000 people, the size of many medieval European cities.

The find has vindicated Fawcett's widely disbelieved claims of a lost city, and while there is much research to be done, the question remains: was this lost civilization the basis for the legend of El Dorado? It is fascinating to note that more than 500 years after Christopher Columbus arrived in the New World searching for gold, the search for the golden city, for a lost paradise, for El Dorado, still continues.

It is perhaps one of our deepest longings—to find new worlds, new civilizations, rich beyond our imagination, with treasures there for the taking. As Jay Robert Nash wrote in his book *Among the Missing*:

> *Deep within most of us lurks the lust for riches. We seek the fabulous treasure troves, or sly business fortunes, or inheritances rendered in the dark. Countless hordes have stalked El Dorado and thousands of other fantasy pits of wealth that subtly encourage the patience and persistence of the seeker on the promise of yielding that inevitable*

pot of gold. The anticipation of discovery is the magic lure, the fine madness in which many have become lost inside their golden pursuits. It is not always a matter of hidden treasure; the motives of these [who pursue so relentlessly] are often vague, sometimes totally inexplicable.

As long as there is a desire for gold, for new lands, mankind will be drawn to it, always in search of El Dorado.

Chronology

1492	Christopher Columbus sails from Spain in search of a direct route to the riches of Asia. Instead, he sails into the New World, landing on what is now the Bahamas on October 12. He made three additional voyages to the New World, opening the way to the discovery of gold and treasure while killing large numbers of the native inhabitants, all the while convinced that he was in Asia, and not the Caribbean, Central, or South America.
1513	Vasco Núñez de Balboa hacks his way across the Isthmus of Darien to become the first European to gaze upon the Pacific Ocean from the New World.
1519	The Spanish found the settlement of Panama, across the Isthmus of Darien, to use as a base to explore the Pacific coasts of Central and South America.
1519	Hernán Cortés, backed by just 450 Spanish soldiers, begins his march on Mexico. By August 1521, the Aztec Empire is in Spanish hands, and its wealth inspires a new flood of want-to-be conquistadors to the New World, all searching for their own empire to conquer.
1529	Ambrosius Ehinger heads the first of two expeditions he will lead on behalf of the Welser Company in search of gold and other treasure. Ehinger ends up getting killed by a poisoned arrow to the neck, and the treasure is lost forever, buried for safekeeping under a tree by a river.
1532	Francisco Pizarro defeats the wealthy Inca Empire, furthering Spanish dreams of yet more golden empires to be discovered and conquered in the New World.
1534	Sebastian de Belalcazar and Pedro de Alvarado arrive in Quito.

1536–1539   Three separate expeditions, led by Sebastian de Belalcazar, Gonzalo Jimenez de Quesada, and Nicholas Federmann, head out through Colombia in search of gold. The one led by Quesada will conquer the Muisca Indians; all three expeditions end up meeting in the Muisca homelands.

1541   Based on the expeditions of Belalcazar, Quesada, and Federmann, stories of El Dorado, of kings covered in golden dust, of religious ceremonies involving sacrifices of gold into a mystical lake, of a land wealthier than any yet discovered, begin to be heard in Quito, and from there spread throughout the New World and Spain.

Timeline

❖ **1492**
Christopher Columbus voyages to the New World, opening the way to the discovery of gold and treasure

❖ **1529**
Ambrosius Ehinger heads the first of two expeditions he will lead on behalf of the Welser Company in search of gold and other treasure

1492

1539

1521
Hernán Cortés, conquers the Aztec Empire, inspiring a flood of would-be conquistadors to the New World, all searching for riches ❖

1532
Francisco Pizarro defeats the wealthy Inca Empire ❖

1536–1539
Three separate expeditions, led by Sebastian de Belalcazar, Gonzalo Jimenez de Quesada, and Nicholas Federmann, head out through Colombia in search of gold ❖

1541	Gonzalo Pizarro, brother of Francisco Pizarro, sets out on the first expedition specifically in search of El Dorado. The expedition will end in failure as Pizarro and his men are forced to turn back in order to survive. A smaller contingent led by Francisco de Orellana, originally sent out in search of food, ends up making history by traveling the length of the Amazon River to its mouth in the Atlantic Ocean.
1580	The first of many attempts is made to drain Lake Guatavita in order to find the golden offerings that the legends say are to be found there. No gold of any major value has ever been found.

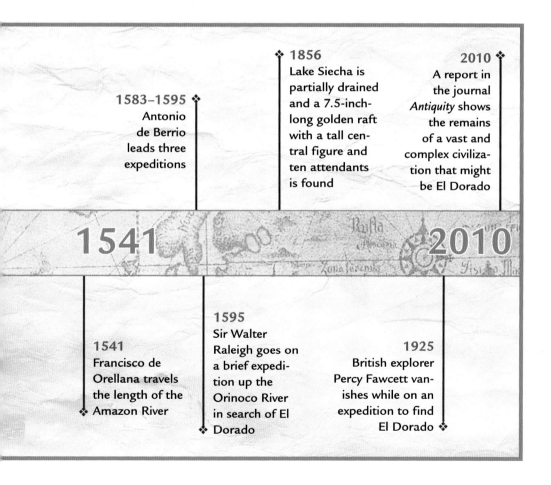

1856
Lake Siecha is partially drained and a 7.5-inch-long golden raft with a tall central figure and ten attendants is found

2010
A report in the journal *Antiquity* shows the remains of a vast and complex civilization that might be El Dorado

1583–1595
Antonio de Berrio leads three expeditions

1541

2010

1541
Francisco de Orellana travels the length of the Amazon River

1595
Sir Walter Raleigh goes on a brief expedition up the Orinoco River in search of El Dorado

1925
British explorer Percy Fawcett vanishes while on an expedition to find El Dorado

1583–1595	Antonio de Berrio leads three expeditions and authorizes others to go on his behalf, in search of El Dorado. All will end in failure.
1595	Sir Walter Raleigh goes on a brief expedition up the Orinoco River in search of El Dorado.
1596	Raleigh publishes *The Discovery of Guinea*, laying out his case for the existence of El Dorado and furthering Europe's fascination with the golden city.
1617	After his release from the Tower of London, Raleigh sails out again in search of El Dorado. The expedition ends in failure with his son killed and his chief lieutenant committing suicide. Raleigh himself will be executed in 1618.
1809	Exploring in the area around Bogota in1809, Alexander von Humboldt visits Lake Guatavita. He notes steps carved into the banks of the lake and calculates that if the tales of sacrifice were true, upward of 50,000,000 golden pieces could still be buried there.
1856	Nearby Lake Siecha is partially drained and a 7.5-inch-long golden raft with a tall central figure and ten attendants is found, setting off speculation that the stories of religious sacrifices of gold are indeed true.
1925	British explorer Percy Fawcett, certain that El Dorado, or, as he refers to it, the city of "Z," is to be found farther south than previously believed, in the Matto Grosso area of Brazil, sets out to find it, accompanied only by his son and his son's best friend. The explorers disappear into the jungle, never to be heard from again.
2010	A report in the journal *Antiquity* by the archeologist Martii Parssinen and others, using satellite imagery, shows the remains of a vast and complex civilization in the very area where Percy Fawcett went out looking for it.

Glossary

Atahuallpa   The last emperor of the Incan empire, he took over the throne in 1522 after defeating his half-brother Huascar in a civil war sparked by the death of their father, Huyana Capac, who most likely died of smallpox introduced by the Spanish conquistadors.

Amazon River   The second longest river in the river with by far the greatest waterflow: One fifth of the world's total river flow winds up in the river's basin.

Conquistador   The term given to those who won the Spanish Empire in the sixteenth century. Although most were Spanish and Portuguese, the first man to whom the term was applied was a Norman, Bethencourt, who conquered some of the Canary Islands starting in 1402.

currency   A medium of exchange. Normally consisting of coins made of valued metals or paper money, in other societies it can be pigs, cacao beans, seashells – whatever is assigned a value by that particular society.

El Dorado   The name of a legendary city or region of the New World, Central or South American specifically, fabled for its gold and jewels. Today, the term is also used for any place that offers fabulous wealth or opportunity.

Great Khan   The westernized title given to the head of the Mongol Empire, which, at its peak, reached from China to Eastern Europe, from India and the Middle East to Siberia.

isthmus   A narrow strip of land forming a link between two larger areas of land – the Isthmus of Panama is perhaps the most famous.

La Malinche   Also known as Malintzin, Malinalli, or Dona Marina, she was a Nahua woman who, acting as interpreter, advisor, lover, and intermediary for Hernando Cortes, played a crucial role in the Spanish conquest of the Aztecs. The mother of Cortes' son, Martin, considered one of the very first Mestizos (people of mixed European and indigenous American ancestry,) she is seen as both traitor and schemer, as well as the mother of the new Mexican people. To this day, the term *malinchista* refers to a disloyal Mexican.

Marco Polo   A Venetian merchant (1254-January 8, 1324), whose twenty four year long journey from Venice to China and back resulted in the book, *The Travels of Marco Polo*. Its descriptions of the fabulous wealth of China and its Great Khan may have helped to inspire Columbus' expedition in search of a western route to China and Japan.

Moors   The term used to describe groups of Berbers, Africans, and Arabs from northern Africa, some of whom conquered and occupied the Iberian peninsula (today's Spain and Portugal) before being defeated by King Ferdinand and Queen Isabella in 1492.

Tenochtitlan   Originally a city-state located on an island in Lake Texcoco. Founded in 1325, it became the capital of the Aztec Empire until it was captured by the Spanish in 1521. Today, the ruins of Tenochititlan are located in the central part, the "centro" of Mexico City.

Bibliography

Aronson, Marc. *Sir Walter Raleigh and the Quest for El Dorado*. New York: Clarion Books, 2000.

Gaffron, Norma. *El Dorado, Land of Gold*. San Diego: Greenhaven Press, 1990.

Grann, David. *The Lost City of Z: A Tale of Deadly Obsession in the Amazon*. New York: Vintage Books, 2010.

Grann, David. "Under the Jungle," *New Yorker*, January 2010. Available online. http://www.newyorker.com/online/blogs/newsdesk/2010/01/the-city-of-z.html.

Hemming, John. *The Search for El Dorado*. London: Phoenix Press, 1978.

Macintyre, Ben. "Hail, Britain's Indiana Jones of the Amazon," *Times of London*, January 7, 2010. Available online. http://www.timesonline.co.uk/tol/comment/columnists/ben_macintyre/article6978417.ece.

Naipaul, V.S. *The Loss of El Dorado: A Cultural History*. New York: Vintage Books, 2003.

Nash, Jay Robert. *Among the Missing: An Anecdotal History of Missing Persons from 1800 to the Present*. New York: Simon and Schuster, 1978.

Severin, Timothy. *The Golden Antille*. New York: Alfred A. Knopf, 1970.

Silverberg, Robert. *The Golden Dream: Seekers of El Dorado*. Athens, Ohio: Ohio University Press, 1985.

Further Resources

Hemming, John. *The Conquest of the Incas*. Boston: Mariner Books, 2003.

Leon-Portillo, Miguel. *The Broken Spears: The Aztec Account of the Conquest of Mexico*. Boston: Beacon Press, 2006.

Nicholl, Charles. *The Creature in the Map: A Journey to El Dorado*. Chicago: University of Chicago Press, 1997.

Time-Life Books editors. *The Search for El Dorado*. New York: Time-Life Books, 1994.

Thomas, Hugh. *Cortes, Montezuma, and the Fall of Old Mexico*. New York: Simon and Schuster, 1995.

Picture Credits

page:
9: Furlong Photography/Alamy
11: Alamy
16: Bridgeman Art Library
21: North Wind Picture Archives/Alamy
25: The Print Collector/Alamy
30: SSPL/Science Museum/The Image Works
35: The Stapleton Collection/Bridgeman Art Library
41: akg-images/The Image Works
44: Robert Harding Picture Library Ltd/Alamy
50: Index/The Bridgeman Art Library
54: Boltin Picture Library/The Bridgeman Art Library
64: Mary Evans Picture Library/The Image Works
73: Prisma Archivo/Alamy
77: Imagestate Media Partners Limited - Impact Photos/Alamy
82: North Wind Picture Archives/Alamy
86: akg-images/British Library/The Image Works
91: Mary Evans Picture Library/The Image Works

Index

About the Author

DENNIS ABRAMS is the author of several books for Chelsea House, including biographies of Barbara Park, Xerxes, Rachael Ray, Eminem, Albert Pujols, and Cotton Mather, as well as books on the Treaty of Nanjing and the history of the automated assembly line. He attended Antioch College, where he majored in English and communications. A voracious reader since the age of three, Dennis lives in Houston, Texas, with his partner of 22 years, along with their three cats and their dog, a basenji named Junie B.